People Interacting

People Interacting

150 Activities to Promote Self Awareness, Communication, Social and Problem-Solving Skills

Ken Hancock and Barry Blaby

Copyright © Ken Hancock and Barry Blaby 2023

All rights reserved. No part of this book may be reproduced or transmitted in any form or by any means, electronic or mechanical, including photocopying, recording or by any information storage and retrieval system, without prior permission in writing from the publisher.

First published in 1990
This second edition was published in 2023

Published by Amba Press
Melbourne, Australia
www.ambapress.com.au

Cover designer – Tess McCabe
Proofreader – Megan Bryant

ISBN: 9781922607546 (pbk)
ISBN: 9781922607553 (ebk)

A catalogue record for this book is available from the National Library of Australia.

Contents

Acknowledgements	vii
Preface	ix
Introduction	1
Planning Grid	14
Warm Ups	19–70
Self Development and Responsibility	71–116
Communication and Relationships	116-158
Groups and Social Skills	152–179
Problem Solving and Decision Making	177–203

People Interacting v

Acknowledgements

Many people contributed to the development of this book over a period of about ten years. It is impossible to name all of the people who have trialled and suggested activities, and who have commented on the format. However, the book was really made possible by the enthusiasm and cooperation of two groups of people studying Humanistic Education at Sturt College of Advanced Education during the late 1970s.

They were Petra Ashton, Margaret Carpenter, Pat Clarke, Yvie Connell, Russ Hubbard, Beth Jeffrey, Emilie Knight, Jan Knox, Rod Kuchel, Colleen Lewis, Murray Maloney, Greg and Judith Manning, Leonie Marnier, Jessie McBride, Syb McCulloch, Colin McGavisk, Graham Ross, Liz Rowe, Jill Hudson, Sara Sims, Dot Tiver, Maria Tumuls and Brigid Weiss. We would like to thank these people especially, for sharing their ideas, activities, resources and energy, and for being prepared to experiment with their own learning.

Although the ideas and activities in this book were compiled by our abovementioned friends and colleagues, the sources of some of the materials were unable to be traced and acknowledged. The authors claim copyright of the arrangement and would appreciate enquiries from persons who believe they hold copyright to any of the material used in this book.

Barry Blaby
Ken Hancock

Preface

This book has been updated for the modern classroom. Activities for self-awareness have been linked with the development of responsibility; other awareness activities have been connected to communication and relationships; group dynamics and role playing have been related to social skills, and problem solving has been linked with classroom decision making.

This book is basically a collection of activities that people have found useful in professional areas, although mostly teaching. It needs to be stressed that activities such as those in this book only take on meaning when placed in some context such as group work in a classroom, content of a curriculum area, or goals in an overall educational program.

The activities are not listed here as the content of a 'new' subject (e.g. Human Relationships) nor as a set of new techniques for amusing people, even though they may be fun in themselves. People using these activities are encouraged to place them into contexts that do make sense to the users. They may be used as aids in achieving traditional classroom goals in basic skills and content (e.g. self-expression in Drama; use of imagination in creative writing; as activities in topics on democracy, prejudice, etc.) or as aids in developing interpersonal skills or group work (e.g. teaching listening skills, cooperation on a project) or as part of a teaching process that is experiential and student centred.

In general, activities should be part of a teaching/learning program that integrates the development of the total person: mind, emotions, body, values and attitudes.

Introduction

The activities in this book have been arranged so that they fit, to some extent, the three priorities of communication, skills for social living and problem-solving skills. The professional task for teachers is to decide how to use these activities in ways that foster the priorities and meet curriculum goals. Many of the activities require structured follow up discussion or processing. It is a very important task for teachers to help students reflect on these activities, and to make sense of them in relation to solving their own problems and developing a positive self concept.

Values and Activities

The activities in this book do not have specific values built into them. However, the moment an activity is used by a teacher it will be given a purpose. This may relate to the content of a lesson, to some point about group work, or to filling in time. And this purpose will contain some value that could be explained to the students. For example, an activity may be run with the purpose of developing listening skills because the teacher values showing respect to others. Sometimes when people run activities, values may be conveyed that are not intended and that are counter-productive. For example, activities may be run by a teacher in a way that always keeps the students dependent on the teacher, even though the teacher may wish to develop self direction in students.

Therefore, it is important for teachers to be clear about the purposes they have for using a specific activity, as well as being clear about the hidden values conveyed by their teaching. Clarifying purposes and implied values is an important step for teachers who may wish to introduce some changes in their teaching priorities, styles or outcomes.

Some of the attitudes and values that have been the foundation for the development of these activities are:
- That thinking and feeling are interrelated processes
- That a positive classroom climate is good for learning: this includes setting clear expectations for behaviour, using student leadership and co-operation, processing classroom activities, and responding to student concerns

- That interpersonal skills are necessarily basic in education and society
- That self direction is valued, along with dependence and interdependence
- That manipulation and exploitation of others is to be discouraged.

Teaching Style and Activities

There is no one way of teaching and learning that suits all teachers and all learners. Hence it is assumed that teachers will develop their own ways of presenting activities, justifying them, relating them to curriculum areas, programming them and using them incidentally as the need emerges.

It is hoped that as teachers begin to use these activities, they will do so with some goal in mind; that they reflect on what they do and that they evaluate their effectiveness. Through developing a way of integrating these activities into one's teaching style, some professional development may begin which will help students and teachers learn and grow together.

Another hope is that people who use these activities will think about doing some in-service education related to this area. Experiencing activities that you will run for others seems to be the best way of understanding the potential value of the activities.

One way of changing professionally, is to choose to do one new action consistently and systematically. Gradually this new behaviour will become integrated into your teaching and will feel like a natural part of your teaching style. Listed below are some practical teaching suggestions, chosen because they seem to support a style of teaching that could suit the activities in this book.

Lesson Planning

Check back on lesson plans. Where you have a cognitive goal only, add a related affective goal (to do with self-awareness, values, attitudes, feelings). Find an activity that will be relevant both to the content (cognitive goals) and the affective goals. Then during the lesson be sure to include discussion of both thoughts and feelings related to content and activity.

Programming

Select a skill to develop each week and set aside a short time each day (10–20 minutes). These skills could include any that occur in the following sections, such as relaxing, responding, listening, planning, setting goals, making 'I' statements.

Teach the skill, using activities, during the 10–20 minutes time, then incidentally include skill practice in content areas of the program for that week.

The Circle Technique

This is a whole class-sharing time, with no wrong answers. The activity is based on the teacher or a student giving a sentence beginning, and the students completing the sentence. As many students as they wish can take turns in completing the sentence. The following should be noted:
- There need to be ground rules such as: one person speaks at a time; all attend to the person speaking; participants can choose to speak or 'pass'.
- Someone (teacher or student) provides an appropriate sentence beginning.
- The teacher can set the pattern for responding by going first until the pattern is established.
- Any contribution is acceptable. There are no wrong answers as participants are expressing their own views and feelings.

Processing

Processing refers to the activity of reflecting on personal, inter-personal and group processes that occur during any interaction. It means examining how people operate rather than what was produced.
- Stop a group (not merely at the end) and have students comment on who is doing what, to whom and with what effect. This means sharing both what went well and what went badly.
- Written responses may be used rather than oral responses.

Processing can be part of the circle technique with sentence beginnings such as:
- I felt it helped when …
- I felt left out when …
- I felt dominated when …
- I felt satisfaction when …
- I felt close to others when …

Group Roles

Assigning group roles can be a beneficial strategy for successful group work. Some ideas to try and include are:

- Draw up a list with students, of positive and negative roles for group members, for example:

    POSITIVE:
    - The *participator* (gets involved)
    - The *idea person* (makes suggestions)
    - The *settler* (helps work out problems)
    - The *fighter* (sticks up for what they believe)
    - The *attention giver* (responds to others)
    - The *checker* (makes sure group knows what's happening)

    NEGATIVE:
    - The *boss* (takes over without considering others)
    - The *troublemaker* (provokes and irritates)
    - The *show-off* (interrupts groups for attention to self)
    - The *stamper* (puts down others' ideas and feelings)
    - The *cop-out* (won't get involved)

- During lessons use the class-developed list to aid recall of how the class functioned.
- Have students share observations in small groups.
- Use an inner and outer circle. The inner circle is the group under observation. Give them a subject to discuss, or a problem to solve. The outer circle gives feedback on the roles different members played.

Dealing with Put Downs

'Put downs' are defined as critical words, statements or actions whose purpose is to hurt the self concept of the victim. People who use put downs are seen as wanting both attention or power over others.

One of the suggestions made for dealing with put downs is to have the put-downer say a sentence such as 'I want to feel powerful right now and I'm doing it at (victim's) expense. Other ways that I can feel powerful are ... ' This may help in thinking about alternatives.

Remember that the point of any of these structures is to build habits (for teacher and student) that will provide a positive climate for helping both learn effectively.

Class Meeting Times

Set aside time for meetings, run democratically, for any of the following purposes:
- To share compliments
- To help each other
- To solve problems
- To plan events.

Initially students will need to be taught the meaning of mutual respect and how to show it, along with the many co-operative group work skills listed later in this book.

Questioning Technique

Examine your current style of questioning. Do you tend to ask questions that are more convergent than divergent, more open ended than closed, more directed at thinking or feeling, more fact, concept, or value oriented? Some questioning techniques may be consistent with the type of processing needed for many of the activities in this book. E.g.

For developing self esteem:
- What do you do well?
- What makes you happy?
- What successes have you had today?

For sharing feelings:
- What kind of things hurt your feelings?
- What makes you feel great?
- How do you feel about this part of your work?

For exploring the processes of a group:
- How included/excluded did you feel today?
- How much influence did each person have?
- What actions helped get the group's task done?

Conflict Resolution

When resolving conflicts between students or when helping students make up their minds about issues, it may be useful to develop some steps that are student-centred. The steps could be used as part of one's style.

Two brief examples of steps are listed below:

Example A

Step 1   Ask student to describe incident.
Step 2   Have student make value judgement about incident.
Step 3   Have student consider alternative actions.
Step 4   Get commitment from student for future behaviour.

Example B

Step 1   Experience
Something happens

Step 2   Identify
Teacher asks:
- 'What happened?'
- 'What are you feeling?'
- 'What did you see?'

Step 3   Analyse
Teacher asks:
- 'Why was that significant?'
- 'What caused that to happen?'
- 'Why did it happen to you?'
- 'What made that important?'
- 'What caused you to feel that way?'

Note: Sometimes people do not know why they did something or why something happened. Because it is less threatening, people may want to re-phrase a 'why' question to a 'What were you wanting to do?' question.

Step 4   Generalise
Teacher asks:
- 'How can you use this?'
- 'How can you do that again under other circumstances?'
- 'How can you do it differently next time?'
- 'What did you learn from the experience?'

Classroom Decision Making – Negotiating Class Rules and Consequences

Developing class rules provides the teacher with the opportunity to model a decision-making process that could be used to solve many problems. Some simple steps in arriving at class rules and consequences could be:
- Have a discussion about the place of rules in different contexts such as home, sport, or on the road.
- Establish the point of having rules e.g. safety, and to help people get along smoothly.
- Notice the consequence of breaking rules. Distinguish between natural and logical consequences, and punishments.
- Have the class, perhaps in small groups, brainstorm possible rules to help people get along well together and learn.
- Collate the rules. (This may be done by the teacher or students.)
- Have the class decide on five or six basic rules.
- Discuss and list the consequences that follow if the rules are broken. (For instance, if a student drops papers on the floor, they should spend some of her own time picking up those papers.)

Organisation of the Activities in this Book

All activities have been placed in one or more of the following categories:
- Warm Ups
- Self Development and Responsibility
- Communication and Relationships
- Groups and Social Skills (including role playing)
- Problem Solving and Decision Making

The next sections outline possible purposes and skills related to activities in each category.

Warm Ups

Warm ups are activities that may be useful when:
- People need to be mixed informally
- People need to relax
- Tension needs to be released
- Physical activity is needed to break a long period of concentration.

Warm ups are useful looseners prior to role playing, group games, problem solving activities or skill learning sessions. In these instances, warm up activities could be chosen because they contain some elements of a skill in an activity to follow.

Obviously, warm ups may be used merely because they are good fun and energising, and no follow up may be necessary. However, some purposes are:
- To help students get to know each other in a variety of ways and situations
- To reduce some social barriers that inhibit the flow of discussion in subjects
- To enable people to become aware of their senses
- To develop a sense of trust and cohesion ('togetherness') in a group
- To develop language for expressing thoughts and feelings.

Skills relating to these purposes that may be developed during warm ups are:
- The ability to join in and participate
- The ability to share reactions (thoughts and feelings)
- The ability to express oneself verbally and non-verbally.

Note: Sharing does not mean invasion of privacy. It means sharing what a person wants to, when ready, as well as discovering those things we have in common.

Teachers may wish to use these activities in other ways. They may be used to reduce unnecessary barriers and tension between students to help produce a positive social climate. They may be integrated with various curriculum areas to produce peer discussion of difficult topics, to increase the possibility of creativity or the use of imagination, and to make learning more experiential.

Self Development and Responsibility
Although schools aim to develop the total person, the development of self concepts usually occur as a biproduct of the curriculum. In placing activities in this category we are not intending to introduce a new curriculum area. Rather, teachers may be able to alter their lesson focus or lesson follow up to ensure greater attention to the development of positive self esteem.

The purpose of activities in this category is to help people know themselves better by moving through a four step process:
- Step 1 increasing self awareness
- Step 2 making sense of the awareness (self understanding)
- Step 3 owning and integrating what one is aware of (self acceptance)
- Step 4 valuing oneself (self esteem).

There are three kinds of awareness that are fundamental to self understanding:
1. Awareness of the outside world: actual sensory contact with objects and events in the present.
2. Awareness of the inside world: what one feels (sensory) inside the skin, e.g. itches, discomfort, dryness in the throat. These are bodily states often related to emotions such as embarrassment or fear.
3. Awareness of cognitive activity: all explaining, imagining, interpreting, guessing, thinking, comparing, planning, remembering the past, anticipating the future. It is mental activity beyond present sensory awareness.

Note: Self awareness activities continue the development of sharing in the warm up activities. It should be stressed that in discussion and processing after an activity, it is important that:
- People are not coerced to share unwillingly, and
- People are listened to and responded to with acceptance.

Skills to be encouraged are:
1. Attending to thoughts: what one says to oneself
2. Attending to feelings: related to feeling a physical sensation under the skin
3. Attending to actions: noticing what I am doing both verbally and non-verbally
4. Expressing awareness by using 'I' statements.

One aid that many find useful in self development is a personal diary or journal. Teachers could set aside time for students to make notes of self expression, not to be read by others (including the teacher). People may then share as much as or as little as they wish.

Teachers' attitudes and expectations while running these activities are also significant. Teachers need to treat students as if they are capable: help students take control over parts of their learning and ask questions that encourage students to make choices. One outcome of being a student should be to feel capable, confident, responsible and with high self-regard. Sharing of experiences, feelings and wants may be encouraged if teachers are prepared to resist making evaluative statements during such discussions.

Communication and Relationships

Being aware of oneself and expressing oneself is part of communication. The complementary part, important for communication and relationships, is being aware of others. 'Other awareness' refers to the ability to perceive accurately the experiences of another person, some call this ability 'empathy'. Most of us act as if we know enough about others not to have to ask whether our assumptions are correct or not. Often our assumptions are not correct and should be checked more frequently.

There are several mechanisms to do with our perception that distort our awareness of others. Projection is one of these. Projection occurs when person A attributes to person B those feelings, motives and thoughts that person A actually has, but may not be aware of having. Self awareness and acceptance help reduce the possibility of projection and blame.

The main skills to emphasise throughout the processing of these activities include:
- The ability to describe behaviour (describe, rather than judge, label and evaluate); e.g. to say 'Jim has made five comments, others have made one', rather than 'Jim is dominating the group'.
- The ability to check out one's perceptions (ask, rather than assume one is correct); e.g. to begin sentences with 'Did I understand you correctly when you said ... ' or 'What I understand you to have said is ... Is that right?'
- The ability to summarise ideas and reflect feelings (called 'active listening'); e.g. 'You feel X (scared) about Y (when the teacher shouts)'.
- The ability to give and receive feedback non-judgmentally and non-defensively, e.g. 'I feel X (really happy) when Y (you say my name and praise my work)'.

Developing these communication skills is fundamental to forming relationships based on mutual respect. Teachers will find the activities and skills valuable when dealing with topics related to friendship, prejudice, caring, co-operation and tolerance. The skills are also useful when dealing with controversial issues of race, peace, sexism, religion etc.

One large part of communication includes non-verbal cues which could be examined when processing activities. Teachers would need to examine their own behaviour to note any discrepancies between their verbal and non-verbal behaviours which may undermine the quality of their relationships with students, colleagues or parents.

Groups and Social Skills

The area of group work includes all of the skills listed in earlier sections. However, role dynamics in a group setting can cause issues to arise, which need to be incorporated into personal and interpersonal skills.

The main purposes of working with people in groups are to teach cooperation and to increase the quality of the learning.

Basic skills for group work include:
- Sharing
- Taking responsibility
- Encouraging others
- Active listening
- Observing and describing behaviour
- Process and comment on what is happening in a group. (e.g. Who has talked and who has not? Who has influenced the group and in what way? Who has been helpful? What feelings have been experienced in the group?)

When teachers begin group work for the first time, both the students and the teacher need to learn new skills of coping. A useful summary of steps needed for the transition from working as a class to working in small groups are:
- Working gradually, learning one step at a time
- Beginning in pairs and teaching students constructive ways of talking and listening
- Also in pairs, learning how to share, take turns and come to agreements
- Moving into larger groups, continuing to practice cooperative skills
- In groups, developing the idea of specific roles (e.g. leader, reporter, encourager) and shared leadership
- Beginning small group work on a task or topic and continuing to process the skills and dynamics.

Role Playing

Groups form a valuable context for developing social skills, and role playing may be used to enable students to act out various situations applying to these social skills. Role playing is a general term referring to acting out scenes, conflicts, feelings, ideas, etc., in a way that people get involved physically, intellectually, and emotionally. Role playing may be either highly structured as described below, or an incidental acting out of situations as they arise.

People who use role playing as part of their teaching style may have the following purposes:
- To develop imagination and creativity
- To develop empathy for others
- To experience new behaviours in a relatively safe situation
- To practice new social behaviours
- To put subject content into a situation that can be experienced fully.

Teachers may use role playing to deal with social problems in school, e.g. anti-social behaviour, cheating, lack of friends, arguments; or they may use role playing to enable students to experiment with different behaviours in particular situations such as running meetings, being a member of a club, coping with peers, and family situations. Role playing is not meant to be uninvolved acting, so the closer the situation is to real life the better the chance of real involvement and learning.

Problem Solving and Decision Making

Problem solving procedures, whether for an individual or group, are closely related to the steps in decision making, and, of course, draw on all of the skills listed in the previous sections.

Basic steps in problem solving are:
1. Defining the problem: checking different understandings
2. Diagnosing the problem: what forces are working for and against a solution
3. Formulating alternative strategies: use creative and divergent options
4. Deciding upon and implementing a strategy: allocate jobs, resources, etc.
5. Evaluating success of a strategy. (If not successful, try another strategy.)

A most important part of education is to learn how to make decisions and choices as an individual and as a member of a group.

Decision making, in general, requires the same steps as problem solving: defining the problem, stating alternative actions, weighing up advantages and disadvantages, and implementing and evaluating a strategy. However, a group may also need to decide how to make a decision, i.e. which method of deciding is more appropriate for the task at hand.

There are seven options available to people making decisions. All have strengths and weaknesses and may be appropriate at different times.
1. Agreement (consensus) of the entire group
2. Majority vote
3. A minority of group members (e.g. an appointed sub-group or executive)
4. Averaging the opinions of group members (usually done after individual consultation by 'leader')
5. Member with most expertise
6. Member with most authority after discussion
7. Member with most authority without discussion.

Teachers may use problem solving steps in many situations. The steps can be used as a discussion/counselling method with individuals, as a conflict resolution method between students or as a method for group projects. Within curriculum areas they may be part of an enquiry method or a way of tackling a project. Also, they may provide a way of coping with personal change. Central to problem solving is the making of judgements related to choices, a basic social skill.

Planning Grid

No.	Activity	Warmups	Self Development/ Responsibility	Communi- cation/ Relationships	Groups/ Social Skills	Problem Solving/ Decision Making
1	Balloon Hit	☑				
2	Group Slime	☑				
3	Feeling	☑		☑		
4	The Machine	☑				☑
5	Crossover Rope Walk	☑				
6	Tunnel Game	☑				
7	Skin the Snake	☑				
8	Duck Shoving	☑		☑		
9	Tripods and Bipods	☑				☑
10	Tangles	☑				☑
11	Hoppa Bumpo	☑		☑		
12	Relays	☑				
13	Caterpillar Walk	☑				
14	Creep Mouse	☑				☑
15	Guard the Goods	☑				☑
16	Balloon Game	☑				
17	Give It a Name	☑			☑	☑
18	Famous Pairs	☑			☑	☑
19	Lateral Thinking	☑			☑	☑
20	Pass the Message	☑				
21	Simple Simon	☑				
22	Thumbs Up	☑				☑
23	Sit and Wink	☑				
24	Pass the Ball	☑				
24	Chin Ball	☑	☑	☑		☑
26	Personal Preference	☑	☑	☑		
27	Mobile Phone Game	☑		☑		
28	Mirror Image	☑	☑		☑	

No.	Activity	Warmups	Self Development/ Responsibility	Communication/ Relationships	Groups/ Social Skills	Problem Solving/ Decision Making
29	I Wrote a Letter	☑				
30	Rhythm Game	☑	☑			
31	Rag Doll, Tin Solider	☑				
32	Hands Have Eyes	☑	☑	☑		☑
33	Introduction Game	☑	☑			
34	Stone Game	☑	☑	☑		☑
35	Memory Picture	☑	☑	☑		☑
36	Secret Messages	☑	☑			
37	Chuckle Belly	☑	☑	☑		☑
38	Don't Rock the Raft	☑		☑		☑
39	Mutual Interview	☑	☑	☑	☑	
40	Jumble	☑		☑	☑	☑
41	Signal Detection	☑	☑		☑	☑
42	Just Relax	☑	☑	☑		
43	Murder	☑	☑	☑		
44	Finding Partners 1	☑				
45	Wring Out the Washing	☑				☑
46	Shut Up and Listen		☑	☑	☑	
47	I Am		☑			
48	Ideal Person		☑	☑		☑
49	Life Line		☑	☑	☑	
50	Heredity/ Environment		☑	☑	☑	☑
51	Who Am I?		☑			☑
52	Coat of Arms		☑		☑	
53	21 Questions		☑		☑	
54	Values		☑	☑	☑	
55	My Bag of Skin		☑	☑		
56	The Timid Teens		☑	☑		
57	Collage		☑	☑	☑	☑
58	Power of Comparison		☑			

No.	Activity	Warmups	Self Development/ Responsibility	Communi- cation/ Relationships	Groups/ Social Skills	Problem Solving/ Decision Making
59	Working for Approval		☑			
60	Life Plan		☑			
61	Win Some/Lose Some		☑			☑
62	Good Feelings		☑	☑	☑	☑
63	Good, Bad and Ugly		☑	☑	☑	☑
64	My Book		☑			
65	I'll Bet You Can't Use		☑			☑
66	Robots		☑			☑
67	Classified Ads		☑	☑		☑
68	Palm Trees, Elephants		☑	☑		
69	Force Choice		☑			☑
70	Feelings Bingo		☑	☑		
71	Relaxation		☑	☑		
72	Wanted		☑			
73	Personality		☑			☑
74	Good Times		☑		☑	☑
75	Every Mother Has One		☑			
76	I'm OK		☑			
77	Childhood Days		☑			
78	Great Day		☑			
79	I Can		☑	☑		
80	Good Feelings		☑		☑	
81	Private		☑		☑	
82	Paint Pot		☑	☑		
83	One Special Thing			☑		
84	Coopers Creek			☑		☑
85	Best Friend			☑		☑
86	Secret Messages			☑		
87	Trusting			☑		
88	Artists and Blobs			☑		
89	Charades			☑	☑	

No.	Activity	Warmups	Self Development/ Responsibility	Communi- cation/ Relationships	Groups/ Social Skills	Problem Solving/ Decision Making
90	Build a Block			☑		☑
91	Fox and Hare			☑		
92	Parent Tapes			☑	☑	
93	Talking Without Words			☑		☑
94	Law of the Jungle			☑		
95	Observation			☑	☑	☑
96	Getting Acquainted			☑		
97	Don't Cry		☑	☑		
98	Rumours			☑		
99	Focus			☑	☑	
100	Helpmate			☑	☑	
101	Film Stars			☑		
102	Clones			☑		
103	Autograph Book			☑		
104	Friends			☑		
105	Ghost Game			☑	☑	☑
106	Families and Friends			☑		
107	Like and Dislike		☑	☑		☑
108	Secret Agent			☑		
109	Table Hunt		☑	☑		
100	Me Cubed		☑	☑		
111	What's Your Name?			☑	☑	
112	Clichés			☑	☑	
113	Journey with Friends			☑	☑	☑
114	Culture Game		☑	☑	☑	☑
115	Ingroups/ Outsiders			☑	☑	
116	Inactive/Passive		☑		☑	
117	Newspapers				☑	
118	Presentation				☑	
119	Ostracising			☑	☑	
120	Building				☑	
121	Apathy		☑		☑	

No.	Activity	Warmups	Self Development/ Responsibility	Communi- cation/ Relationships	Groups/ Social Skills	Problem Solving/ Decision Making
122	Co-operate			☑	☑	☑
123	Straw Game				☑	☑
124	Prepared Argument				☑	
125	Today		☑		☑	
126	Group Works				☑	☑
127	Telegram Ti-Tree			☑	☑	
128	Smilo				☑	
129	Finding Partners 2		☑	☑	☑	☑
130	Co-operation		☑	☑	☑	☑
131	What Am I?		☑	☑		☑
132	Role Plays		☑		☑	☑
133	Roads/Avenues					☑
134	Scissor Game		☑			☑
135	Best Job					☑
136	Predicament					☑
137	Newspaper Costume					☑
138	Bomb Shelter		☑			☑
139	Passenger Balloon		☑			☑
140	Life Boat		☑			☑
141	Jury Service		☑			☑
142	Lottery Week		☑			☑
143	Dear Heart Mender		☑			☑
144	Personal Survey		☑	☑		☑
145	Do It				☑	☑
146	Grey Power				☑	☑
147	Camp Plan				☑	☑
148	Animal Crackers				☑	☑
149	Buzz Off				☑	☑
150	Teacher For a Day		☑	☑	☑	☑

1
Balloon Hit

Focus
Warm up

Time
Between 10 to 15 minutes

Materials
- One balloon, inflated

Procedure
Everyone stands in a large circle. Hit a balloon into the air and keep it aloft for as long as possible. No person may hit the balloon twice in a row. The balloon may not touch the floor. The person who allows the balloon to hit the floor is to share some information about themselves with the group.

2
Group Slime

Focus
Warm up

Time
About 5 minutes

Procedure
Lie in a circle on the floor as far from the centre of the room as possible with all heads toward the centre. With eyes closed, slowly crawl into the centre forming a pile, then cross to the other side of the room.

3
Feeling

Focus
Warm up

Time
About 10 minutes

Materials
- Speakers with the ability to play music

Procedure
Play music of various styles. Everyone in the group, with eyes open, acts out their feelings in dance.

Variation
1. All standing in circle, eyes closed body stiff
2. Play music softly
3. Leader instructs group to move hands; then arms; then head, leading to a loosening of all body parts.

4
The Machine

Focus
Warm up

Time
About 5 minutes

Procedure
Participants are to become parts of a large imaginary machine. One person acts out repetitive motion and sound of a machine part. One by one, other parts are added to the machine until the whole group is involved, for example:
- The starter
- A wheel
- Pistons
- Moving handle
- Stamper
- Whirligig

Variation
- One person chooses persons to act as parts of the machine.

5
Crossover Rope Walk

Focus
Warm up

Time
10 minutes

Materials
- Length of rope, about 3m

Procedure
Place a rope on the floor or hold it taut up to 30cm above the ground, depending on the ability of participants. Players start at one end of the rope with both feet on one side of the rope facing the other end of the rope. The outer foot is moved to the other side of the rope. The other foot is then moved round the first foot and placed on the other side of the rope from the first foot, the outer edge again resting alongside the rope. This is continued until the player reaches the other end of the rope.

Variation
One person takes the rope and makes it into something (e.g. a boat, wings of an aeroplane, a supermarket shelf, a manhole cover). The next, guesses what it is by the actions of the person (e.g. sitting down, rowing, etc.)

6
Tunnel Game

Focus
Warm up

Time
5 minutes

Procedure
Players line up facing each other (2 rows). All kneel down placing hands on shoulders of opposite partner. This forms a tunnel. Other players crawl through the tunnel then kneel and form new tunnel until all players have had a turn.

7
Skin the Snake

Focus
Warm up

Time
15 minutes

Materials
- Length of rope, about 3m

Procedure
Players stand in single file with their legs slightly apart and place their right hand between their legs. With their left hand they grasp the right hand of the person in front of them. Once the snake is formed the tail member lies down on their back with their legs between the person in fronts legs. The snake then moves slowly backwards, players still with joined hands at all times. When a player reaches the head of the person lying down they in turn lie down on their back with one leg either side of the person, lying in front of them, still holding hands. When all players are lying down but still holding hands, the last person to lie down stands up and very slowly starts to walk to the front of the snake pulling the next person to their feet. This continues until all players are again in their original starting positions.

Note: This activity requires appropriate clothing, same sex groups and a meaningful context e.g. Dance or Drama.

8
Duck Shoving

Focus
Warm up

Time
5 minutes

Procedure
Players pair up and squat facing each other. The object of the exercise is to make the other person fall over whilst remaining in a squatting position. This may be achieved by gently pulling or pushing the other person or by avoiding their lunges.

9
Tripods and Bipods

Focus
Warm up

Time
5 minutes

Procedure
Participants, with appropriate clothing, stand with legs apart and bend forward until their hands are on the floor. The leader then asks them to lift one hand or one foot off the floor (thereby forming a tripod). Once each of the four limbs has been individually raised and replaced, the participants are asked to raise one arm and one leg at the same time.

Variation
Participants stand with two body parts touching the ground (e.g. standing), then 3 body parts (e.q., 2 knees and an elbow).
Try 4, 5, 6 body parts.

10
Tangles

Focus
Warm up

Time
15 minutes

Procedure
Stand in circle, holding hands. Hands must not be let go!

Have a leader tie the circle up in knots by going under, over, around each other, holding hands all the time. Once the circle is tied up, then try to untangle without breaking hands; this involves quite a lot of patience and co-operation.

Variation
One person to go out of the room while the group tangles itself. When the person returns they have to untangle the group.

11
Hoppo Bumpo

Focus
Warm up

Time
10 minutes

Materials
- Piece of chalk

Procedure
Draw a circle on the floor of diameter about 1.5 metres. Two players pair up, and stand facing one another in the circle. Each player stands on his/her left foot, and grasps the right foot behind his/her back with the left hand. The right arm should be bent across the body to grasp the left shoulder. Each player attempts to gently bump the other out of the circle by hopping on the left foot and bumping with the body. The winner is the player who moves the other out of the circle, or makes them put both feet down, or fall on the floor.

12
Relays

Focus
Warm up

Time
10 minutes

Procedure
These depend very much on the room available. However, restricted space can be used effectively if the running is made more difficult by such procedures as: Forming teams of equal numbers. Travelling sideways on all fours, with the hands crossing over with each step; rabbit hopping by springing from a crouching position with the hands being cupped, palms forward, on the head like rabbit ears; spider walking by going, with back downwards, and moving on all fours, backwards. Crab walking is the same as spider walking, but moving sideways.

13
Caterpillar Walk

Focus
Warm up

Time
10 minutes

Procedure
Each person lies on his/her stomach with arms straight out in front. The feet are then 'walked' up to the hands (ideally with the knees being kept straight). The hands are then walked forward to the extended position. The process is repeated over the required distance. The hands and feet are never moved at the same time.

14
Creep Mouse

Focus
Warm up

Time
15 minutes

Materials
- Blindfold

Procedure
Players form as large a circle as possible in the room with one member standing blindfolded in the middle. Each person in the circle is a mouse and, one at a time, creeps towards the cat. As soon as the blindfold cat hears a sound they point in that direction. If the cat points at the advancing mouse it must stop where it is and sit down. The next mouse then creeps forward until detected by the cat. If a mouse succeeds in reaching the cat undetected, they then change roles and all mice go to the perimeter.

15
Guard the Goods

Focus
Warm up

Time
10 minutes

Materials
- Blindfold

Procedure
The group forms a large circle with a guard sitting blindfolded and cross-legged in the centre with the goods (e.g. a packet of sweets) in front of them. One at a time the players creep forward and try to remove the goods without being touched by the guard. Any player who is touched must return to the circle.

16
Balloon Game

Focus
Warm up

Time
10 minutes

Materials
- Balloons (one per person), string, scissors

Procedure
After distributing one balloon and string to each person, instruct each person in the group to blow up their balloon and tie it to their ankle. Once all balloons are in place, tell the group to burst as many balloons belonging to other people as possible, and to sit down when their balloon has been burst. Sit down when your balloon has been burst. This activity is better when no-one is wearing shoes.

17
Give It a Name

Focus
Warm up

Time
20 minutes

Procedure
1. Present a short story of your choice or the one below, expanding it with further details and explanation, as necessary.

   Story
   Some countries in the world have tough drug laws. One Australian woman was caught smuggling cannabis into Indonesia. She was put on trial, convicted and sentenced to 20 years in prison. Publicly she maintained that the drugs had been planted in her body bag without her knowledge. After many appeals for clemency, she was granted a 5 year reduction and returned to Australia having served 15 years in prison.

2. Form groups of 2 or more. Using only words beginning with any of the letters w... c... e... n... d... p..., in any order, how many different titles can groups produce for the story?
3. In the class, read out and discuss the appropriateness of the titles.

18

Famous Pairs

Focus
Warm up

Time
10 minutes

Materials
- Small pieces of card, felt pen, pins

Procedure
Prepare a number of small cards using pairs of names, with one name on each card. Use names that suit your group. E.g.
- Antony and Cleopatra
- Superman and Lois Lane
- Peter Pan and Wendy
- Batman and Robin
- Beyoncé and Jay-Z
- Mickey Mouse and Minnie Mouse
- Donald Duck and Daisy Duck

Shuffle the cards. Each person pins one on the back of another person, without revealing the name. Everyone has to walk around the room, without speaking or signalling, and use detective work to find their partner.

Variation
Each person acts the role of the person whose name is pinned on their back, as an aid to their partner.

19
Lateral Thinking

Focus

To increase awareness of a range of possible responses to statements

Time

15 minutes or longer

Procedure
1. Select five of the following listed items:
   - Eight uses for a rubber band
   - Four ways to start an argument
   - Nine things that make you happy
   - Five ways to put off doing things
   - Six people that you'd lend money to
   - Seven ways to learn things
   - Three ways to ride a bicycle
   - Five ways to relax
   - Two ways to pat a dog
   - Three ways to make people laugh
2. People work alone listing as many as they can.
3. Share responses in groups of four.
4. Option: each group chooses its most unusual response for sharing with whole class.
5. Prepare more lateral thinking exercises. Plan an activity using lateral thinking procedures. Let your imagination go wild.

Discussion
- What stops people from using their creative imaginations?

20
Pass the Message

Focus

Personal contact at a minimal level and non-verbal awareness

Time

15 minutes or as required

Materials

- Small pieces of card, felt pen, pins

Procedure

1. Everyone sits in circle except for one person who sits in the centre with their eyes closed.
2. Everyone links their little fingers.
3. One person is chosen to 'pass the message' and one chosen to 'receive' it.
4. The person in the middle opens their eyes.
5. The 'message' is then passed by squeezing the little finger of the person next in line without being seen by the person in the middle. The squeeze must be passed on from person to person without the person in the middle spotting the squeeze.
6. If the message gets around the circle, the person next to the starter says 'message received', and the game ends.

Note: Hands must be in full view all of the time.

Variation

1. A 'starter' is chosen. They say 'I am going to pass a message to … on the other side of the circle'. They can send the message either to the left or to the right. The person in the centre must try and catch someone squeezing.
2. One person sits in the middle with eyes closed. A starter is chosen from the circle and they start a message around the circle to themselves. The middle person opens their eyes and attempts to find someone currently sending the message and who started it.

3. Send the message by touching
   - Elbows
   - Shoulders
   - Knees
   - Heads.

Discussion
- Discuss in a group. Is it less embarrassing to hold someone's little finger or someone's hand? Say why or why not!
- Did you notice the expressions that people had on their faces while passing the message? If you didn't, play the game again. Discuss the reasons for the expressions, or lack of them.
- Discuss the expression 'poker face'. What is the reason people use a 'poker face'? What is the opposite of a 'poker face'? Find some magazine pictures of both, cut them out and paste them on a large sheet.

21
Simple Simon

Focus
Using the senses – hearing and seeing

Time
10 minutes or longer

Procedure
1. Everyone stands in a line except one person who stands in front of the group.
2. They calls out things to do.
3. Everyone must do what the person at the front says provided they say 'Simple Simon' first e.g. 'Simple Simon says sit down!' (They must sit down). 'Sit down!' (They must not sit down).
4. The game keeps going until there is only one person left. They are the winner.
5. A person is out if they do something when the person at the front has not said 'Simple Simon' first.

Variation
The person at the front must perform the action they say, whether they say 'Simple Simon' first or not.

Discussion
- At the end of each game, talk about anything you have learned from the lesson. How do listening and looking help or hinder each other? What are you going to do about what you have learnt?
- Talk about situations where other people try to trick you into doing things.
- Discuss some other ways that people get you to do things e.g. 'I'll give you 20c if you will go to the shop for me.' Or 'If you don't ... , I'll bash your head in.' Give examples of your own.

22
Thumbs Up

Focus
Body contact at a minimal level and tactile awareness

Time
10 minutes

Procedure
1. Choose 3 or 4 persons to stand in front of the class.
2. Each person in the class closes their eyes and holds their thumb up in the air.
3. The people from the front go amongst the class and hold one or two of the thumbs for a few seconds, then return to the front of the class.
4. The members of the class open their eyes on signal and attempt to choose who of the 3 or 4 persons touched their thumb.

Discussion
- How did you ascertain who touched you?
- How could you make the game easier? Harder?

23
Sit and Wink

Focus
Physical contact at a minimal level and visual awareness

Time
10 minutes or as necessary

Materials
- 6–8 chairs

Procedure
1. Place some chairs in a circle, about 6 or 8.
2. One person sits on each chair, leaving one empty chair.
3. One person stands behind each of the chairs with both their hands on the back of the chair.
4. The person standing behind the empty chair has to wink at someone, sitting.
5. The person winked at, has to race to the empty chair without the person behind grabbing them and holding them securely. Persons standing behind the chair cannot move from the position.

Discussion
- How easy or difficult is it to pay attention to and notice non-verbal behaviour? Share examples.

24
Pass the Ball

Focus
Feelings recall and discussion

Time
10 minutes

Materials
- Large rubber ball/soccer ball/basketball

Procedure
1. Everyone sits in a circle.
2. One person goes into the middle and closes their eyes.
3. The people in the circle then start passing the ball around.
4. When the person in the middle calls 'stop', the ball must stop moving.
5. Before the person in the middle looks up, the person with the ball says a letter of the alphabet.
6. The person who has the ball then passes the ball around the circle while the person in the centre tries to say 6 words beginning with that letter before the ball gets back to the 'starter'.
7. If they fail, choose another person to go into the middle. If they succeed, they stay.

Variation
Vary the number of words to make the game easier or harder.

Discussion
- What were your feelings when the ball was nearly around the circle and you hadn't thought of the correct number of words? Did you feel silly? What do you think the others in the circle felt about you? Ask them!
- Talk about the things that confused you when you were trying to think of words.
- What can you do to stop getting yourself confused? E.g. don't look at the ball as it goes around.
- Is it better not to go in the game, rather than lose?

25

Chin Ball

Focus
Personal contact

Time
10 minutes

Materials
- Tennis ball

Procedure
1. Everyone sits in a circle.
2. Pass the ball around the circle (with hands).
3. Now pass the ball around using only the left hand.
4. Now sit on left hand and pass the ball around the circle with the right hand.
5. Then pass the ball around using only feet.
6. If appropriate, now put the ball under the chin and pass it around.
7. If one person drops the ball, it goes back one and is passed to that person again.

Discussion
- Discuss how you felt when you had to pass the ball with your hands, compared with when you had to stand up close and pass with your chin.
- Did you feel uncomfortable being closer than normal to someone?
- Did it make a difference if the person was a friend or not?

26
Personal Preference

Focus
Personal contact and disclosure

Time
15 minutes

Procedure
1. Group to sit on chairs in a circle with one person standing in the centre. The person in the centre tells the others what they like first and dislike second. E.g. I like people wearing silver rings, but I don't like people wearing blue jumpers (or who smoke or who pick their noses etc.).
2. All those who identify with the negative statement (i.e. those wearing blue jumpers) must stand up and change seats with someone else wearing a blue jumper.
3. The person in the centre also attempts to find an empty seat first. This leaves another person in the centre and the process is repeated.

Try to choose things you really like, and really dislike.

Discussion
- Did some of the likes and dislikes of other people annoy you, or please you? Discuss this.
- Make a whole group list of likes and dislikes. See if you can all agree on some.

27
Mobile Phone Game

Focus
Using the senses – listening and speaking and imagination

Time
15 minutes

Procedure
1. Everyone sits in a circle.
2. The first person picks up an imaginary mobile phone and starts a conversation, two or three phrases long, with an imaginary person on the other end of the line.
3. They then pass the mobile phone around to the person on their right. That person must continue the conversation with two phrases in response to what the imaginary person could have said.
4. Continue around the group, for example:
   P1 'Hello, is that you John? Well, how are you now? Any better?' (pass the mobile phone)
   P2 'That's good! I hope your arm doesn't have to be in plaster long.' (pass the mobile phone)
   P3 'Good! At least I bet you learned one thing from riding that fast.' (pass the mobile phone)

Variation
1. Use a theme for the conversation, e.g. going shopping.
2. Record the conversation. Replay and share alternative responses.
3. Two people put their hands in a sock to make a puppet and kneel on the floor facing one another across a table. Now let the puppets talk to one another; sometimes about each other and sometimes about the person whose hand is in the sock. Say some good things and talk about things that bother you.

Discussion
- Sometimes it's easier to talk to someone through text message on a mobile rather than face to face. Give examples and discuss what makes it easier (or harder).
- Imagine you have broken a window. Is it easier to text or phone the owner and tell them? Which would be the better thing to do? Why?

28
Mirror Image

Focus
Accurate observation and self image

Time
20 minutes

Procedure
1. Divide into pairs, 'A' and 'B', and stand or sit facing one another.
2. 'A' is the person looking into a mirror. 'B' is the mirror.
3. 'A' must do some movements and 'B' has to copy them exactly, and at the same time, as though 'B' is the mirror image of 'A'.
4. The idea is to begin slowly and do everything precisely. Some ideas for movements are looking into the mirror in the morning (e.g. combing hair, brushing teeth, washing face).
5. 'A' and 'B' then change roles.

Variation
1. Do things more quickly or slowly depending on how 'B' can keep up.
2. Make up an act to show another group of people.
3. Work in 4s.
4. Form two groups. Each group elects a leader. The 2 leaders face each other with a dividing line between them. They must not cross over this line. Their respective groups line behind them. The leaders do movements that show action and reaction. The groups mirror the movements of their leaders.
   - Can be done in pairs.
   - Can be done to drum beat/music.
5. Choose one person to stand in the centre of a circle of people with their eyes closed. The circle moves slowly around until the person in the centre calls stop. They then move towards someone in the circle and try to identify that person by feeling their face. Repeat.

Discussion

- How do you feel about looking at yourself in a mirror? Has anybody ever told you not to keep looking at yourself in the mirror? What does 'vanity' mean? Can you look at yourself in the mirror without being vain?
- Find a mirror and look carefully at yourself. Are your ears and eyes the same size; same colour; same shape; same height? Study carefully the freckles and any other features of your face. Make faces at the mirror. Can you make your face look like that of some famous person, or animal? Write on a piece of paper the good things about your face. Then write down the things that you would like to change about your face. Can you change anything about your face? Can you do anything to improve it? Most people just have to live with the faces they have.
- What did it feel like to have someone else's hands over your face? What would be an alternative way of playing this game? Can you think of situations where other people would have to touch your face? Discuss possible feelings these situations may evoke.

29
I Wrote a Letter

Focus
Using and refining the senses

Time
10 minutes

Procedure
1. Everyone sits in a circle.
2. One person gets a handkerchief, a shoe or another object and walks slowly around the outside of the circle. While they do that, the others close their eyes and sing/chant/repeat this song –
'I wrote a letter to my love and on the way I dropped it, someone must have picked it up and put it in their pocket.'
3. When they are ready, the person on the outside quickly drops the object he is holding on to the floor behind somebody and begins to run around the circle.
4. The person picks up the object from behind them and runs after the 'dropper'.
5. The dropper must try to get to the chaser's home spot before he does. If they do, they are safe. If, however, the chaser catches the dropper, they repeat the game.

Variation
Instead of run: skip, hop, crawl, run backwards, slither.

Discussion
- Find out how this game got its name. How could you make the game more difficult?
- What senses did you use most during this game? Did you feel yourself straining? Which senses do you use most during the day? Make a list of the senses, and put them in order of the amount you use them. Take the senses that you don't use much. What things can you do to develop them more? Can a blind person hear better than a sighted one? What things can you do to develop your most used senses more?

30
Rhythm Game

Focus
Accurate listening

Time
15 minutes

Procedure
1. Everyone sits in a circle.
2. Four people are named Matthew, Mark, Luke and John. Or use any four popular one or two syllable names. All the rest are given numbers, beginning from one.
3. Everyone starts clapping a rhythmic beat, about one a second.
4. The person who is Matthew starts off saying Matthew, Matthew, Matthew, Matthew, keeping in time, and then says the name or number of any of the other students e.g. Matthew, Matthew, Matthew, Matthew, 4. In that case the person who is the number 4 says their number four times, in time with clapping, and then calls another name or number, all the time keeping in time with the clapping.
5. The only way to get out is to miss a beat or to not keep in time with the clapping, e.g., Matthew, Matthew, Matthew, Matthew 4; 4, 4, 4, 4 – Mark; Mark, Mark, Mark, Mark – Luke; Luke, Luke, Luke, Luke – 16 etc.

Variation
1. Clap slower or faster.
2. Give everyone their own name or a new name.
3. Everyone has the name of the person next to them.

Discussion
- How did you feel when you missed out, and when you succeeded? When you missed, what do you think the others were thinking? Ask them! Were they thinking how silly you were or were they worrying about whether they would miss a turn?
- Recall what was happening physically to you while you were waiting to see if your number was called. Were you tense? Muscles tight? What were you doing with your hands? Tell others in the group about other times when this same thing happened. Can you stop getting excited? Do you want to? Can you think of other occasions when you got excited and didn't feel well, or you felt upset?

31
Rag Doll, Tin Soldier

Focus
Body contact activities, giving and following directions

Time
10 minutes each activity

Procedure

Activity 1
1. Choose who will be A and who B. In the first round A's will be tin soldiers and B's will be their directors. Tin soldiers can only move under directions from B. They have no power to think or make decisions.
2. Tin soldiers walk slowly with stiff legs and arm joints, obeying only the direct orders of B.
3. B's job is to guide their tin soldier to a seat on the other side of the room by giving directions, and turning them so as to avoid hitting walls, tables, and other tin soldiers walking around the room. Now have the B's switch on their tin soldiers and begin giving directions.
4. After a few minutes stop the action and reverse roles.

Activity 2
1. A's are to be on their backs on the floor. They are to become totally limp like rag dolls. B's job is to try and lift them to their feet. (Be careful not to strain your back.)
2. After a few minutes reverse the roles.

Discussion
- How did you feel? Was it fun? What did you do?
- Was it easier to be the tin soldier than the leader? Or the rag doll?
- What were your feelings as you tried to lift the rag doll?

Activity 3
1. Choose partners and have them designate themselves A and B.
2. A is to act as the sculptor and B the clay. A's job is to mould B into a statue that expresses how A is feeling right now.
3. When this is done ask the B's to tell the A's how they imagine they must be feeling.
4. After a few minutes reverse the process.

32
Hands Have Eyes

Focus
Using the senses: touching in different ways

Time
30 minutes

Materials
- Blindfold

Procedure
1. Everyone stands in a circle. No one must speak.
2. One person is chosen to go in the middle and is blindfolded.
3. The other people then move around clockwise or anti-clockwise in the circle. They stop when the person in the middle says 'stop'.
4. The person in the middle walks out of the circle and tries to identify the first person they come to, by touch only.
5. If they identify them correctly the game starts again with the same person in the middle.
6. If they don't identify them correctly, then the person not identified goes into the middle and is blindfolded to start the game again.

Variation
1. Touch only faces and heads. Or only feet or shoes. Or only hands.
2. Persons in the circle can make a little noise of their own to help identification.
3. Touch with only one hand, or one finger.

Discussion
- Discuss how different touches mean different things. A pat on the back sometimes means 'You have done a good thing'. What can holding hands mean?
- Who touches you most? Your mother, father, friend, grandmother, etc.? How do you feel when someone touches you? Does it make a difference who it is and where it is?
- Choose somebody in the room. See how close you can stand to them without touching them before they move away. Discuss 'personal space'.

33

Introduction Game

Focus

A memory improvement activity, linking names with other situations

Time

10 minutes

Materials

- Pencil

Procedure

1. Everyone sits in a circle.
2. One person holds up a pencil (named Peter) and introduces Peter and themself (Doug) to the person on their right, saying 'This is Peter and I am Doug, who are you?' They then hand the pencil on to the next person on their right (Barry) who introduces everybody to the person on their right (Mary), by saying, 'This is Peter (holds up the pencil), this is Doug (points to Doug), I am Barry, who are you?'
3. The game continues until the whole group is introduced to the one who started (Doug).

Variation

1. When you introduce yourself, you must say what your favourite animal is as well, e.g. 'This is Peter, my name is Doug and my favourite animal is a donkey'. Tom then says, 'This is Peter and that is Doug and their favourite animal is a donkey, and my name is Tom, and my favourite animal is a monkey'. They then pass on the pencil.
2. Shake hands with each person as you are introduced.

Discussion

- Say how you felt when a person you were being introduced to did not smile or say hello to you. How did you feel when they did seem pleased to meet you?
- Work out some ways you might get to meet a certain person, if you didn't know anybody who could introduce you.
- Work in three's. Get one person to introduce one person to another. In one case have both partners smiling. In another case have only one smiling and the other poker face. In another case have neither of them smiling. Discuss how each person felt in the different situations.

34
Stone Game

Focus
To increase awareness and allow physical contact between people, each other and the environment

Time
30 minutes

Materials
- A collection of small stones of different shapes and colours

Procedure
This game is suitable for any number, from a small group of four upwards. Each player will need to choose a stone.
1. Select a stone.
2. Sit in groups of about twelve, facing inwards in a circle.
3. Really get to know the stone you have chosen so that you will be able to identify it. Blindfolded, or with closed eyes, pass all stones around the circle and stop when you think you have your own stone returned.

Discussion
- What factors helped or hindered in identifying your stone?

35
Memory Picture

Focus
Accurate observation, interpretation or projection

Time
25 minutes

Materials
- Pencils, paper, chairs

Procedure
1. Everyone finds a partner.
2. Get a pencil, a piece of paper and a chair.
3. Each person sits directly opposite their partner.
4. They look at each other for one minute.
5. They then turn back to back and draw each other, and write down:
   - 5 things their partner is wearing
   - 5 things about what kind of person their partner is.
6. Turn around, sit alongside your partner and show her your drawing and lists. Check for what is correct. Explain to your partner why you wrote what you did.

Variation
Write down a list of all the qualities you think you have. Give the list to your partner who will tick the ones they agree with. They should be able to give examples as to why they ticked, or did not tick, an item on the list.

Discussion
- Work in groups of four. Look through magazines and find pictures of people. Cut them out, paste them on a piece of paper and then write underneath the picture how your group thinks the person is feeling: angry, sad, happy, wistful, etc. Point out on the picture the things which make you think the person is feeling angry, or sad, etc.
- Can you tell how a person is feeling by the way they look? Always? How can you check?

- Work in groups. One person should get a tray and put about 15 different small things on it. Show the others in the group for one minute, put the tray away and get the rest of the people in the group to write down the name of as many of the things on the tray as they can. Discuss things which help you remember better.
- Work in pairs. Tell your partner something that always makes you mad; perhaps someone calling you a horrible name. Sit opposite your partner and have them say your nickname in a taunting fashion to you over and over until you feel yourself getting angry. Stop, then both sit back in your chairs, close your eyes and 'listen' to your body. Feel which muscles are tight and strained. Concentrate on one part of your body at a time and see if you can relax it. If you can, it was tense. You might find that your whole body is tense in anger. Role play other feelings such as happiness or sorrow. Feel which parts of your body are affected. (All those who can't find anything that makes them mad can be observers.)
- Discuss this statement: 'If you are relaxed, you can't get angry.'

36
Secret Messages

Focus
Using the senses: listening and imagining

Time
30 minutes

Procedure
1. Form a group and sit in a circle.
2. One person makes up a verse, or a sentence, e.g. The cat went to see the Queen.
3. That person then whispers the statement to the person on their right, clearly but softly so that the other people cannot hear them. That person then whispers the verse to the person on their right and so on until the verse has reached the person who started it.
4. The first person then stands up and repeats the verse as they receive it from the person next to them.
5. If the verse has changed, the first person starts another round, with a different statement.
6. If it has not, the organiser picks another person to begin the next round.

Discussion
- Do we always listen exactly to what is said to us? If not, why not? Talk about a time when someone didn't listen to what you said.
- Are there times when it is OK to whisper in someone's ear? If so, when?
- Can you tell when somebody is whispering about you? Or, can you only guess that they are? How could you find out if they were whispering about you?
- How do you feel if you think somebody is whispering to someone else about you? Talk about a time this happened. Can you remember a time when you were talking to someone and somebody else thought you were talking about them? What happened?

37
Chuckle Belly

Focus
Personal body contact, and personal space

Time
10 minutes

Procedure
The organiser says, 'See if you can all make a circle so that everyone's head is on someone else's stomach.' When everyone has worked out how to make the circle, the organiser then chooses somebody in the group. They lie down alongside that person and cracks a joke in their ear. They will giggle. When the next person feels the giggle they will giggle, and it will pass right around the circle.

Variation
The organiser chooses somebody to giggle or cough and directs the next person to pass it on around the circle.

Discussion
- Look at this list and decide for yourself which statement applies to you.
    - I felt uncomfortable when I had to lie on someone else's stomach
    - I felt very cosy when I had to lie on someone else's stomach
    - I felt OK when I had to lie on someone else's stomach.
- Work in pairs, A and B. Face one another. A walks towards B very slowly, face to face, until A is 'too close for comfort' for B. B says stop. Measure the distance. This distance is a measure of B's personal space. Check your own personal space (the distance you like people to be away from you). Discuss the things that alter the area of your personal space, e.g.
    - Allowing your best friend to come closer
    - Keeping a stranger further away.
- Find reasons for a large personal space. How necessary is it? How can you change it, if you want to? Observe people talking together. Does personal space change with the situation? Get a rough estimation of human personal space from observing other people talking together.

Note: This activity may need to be done in appropriate clothing and same sex groups.

38
Don't Rock the Raft

Focus
Group awareness and co-operation

Time
15 minutes

Materials
- Pencils, paper, chairs

Procedure
1. Establish an area to be used to represent a raft, which must be balanced by people being spread evenly otherwise it will sink!
2. Establish correct stance. Think of the head as a helium balloon, pulling the body upright. The pelvis is a weight to keep the body from flying up. Arms hang loose.
3. Play music. Keeping correct stance and remembering to balance the raft, walk around the area, being careful not to touch anyone.
4. While music is still playing, double the walking pace (remembering all the time to keep correct posture, balance raft and not touch).
5. Practise changing tempo from double, to half, to normal pace, keeping all other requirements.
6. Once the group is able to change tempo, ask everyone to go at normal pace and introduce change of direction (backwards, to the left, to the right, forwards).
7. Combine change of direction and pace, e.g. walk backwards at normal pace … now to the left at half pace etc. keeping all other requirements at the same time.
8. Once the group is able to change tempo and direction and also balance the raft, keep correct posture and not touch, introduce the idea of watching each other carefully so that everyone changes without formal or verbal directions.
9. It may be necessary, at first, depending on the group, to ask one person to be responsible for changing pace/tempo and the rest of the group must watch and change.
10. Eventually it should be possible for the group to have no set leader nor any individual to change tempo and/or direction.

11. Points to watch:
    - Set a time limit of at least half a minute of one pattern of tempo and direction before anyone changes it.
    - Emphasise that is a group activity and it is necessary to watch carefully.

Discussion
- How often did you try to change the pattern?
- Did you notice just one or two people always changing the pattern, or were there many different people changing the pattern?
- What happened if more than one person tried to change the pattern at once?

39
Mutual Interview

Focus
Useful for establishing group cohesion and starting new groups or classes

Time
30 minutes

Procedure
1. Divide group into As and Bs.
2. A takes a B partner and goes away for a private interview.
3. The interviewer must find out as much about that person as possible in five minutes.
4. Both return to the group and A introduces partner B to the group and gives a short introductory speech about them.

Variation
The group discusses a number of controversial questions and they are written down:
- Marijuana smoking is good/bad for you.
- Divorce is beneficial/harmful to society.
- Marriage is wonderful/a waste of time.
- Dogs are 'man's best friend'/darned nuisances.

Each partner speaks for two minutes either for or against the subject. The other partner has to take the opposite point of view. They begin by stating A's point of view, then states their opposite point of view.

Discussion
- Are people happy to tell you about themselves?
- Did you agree with what the other person said? About you? About the topic?
- Did it make you annoyed? Were you annoyed that they didn't like what you said?
- How can you get the other person to agree with you?
- What does it mean to "agree to differ" with someone?

40

Jumble

Focus
Body contact and feelings

Time
30 minutes: four players and a person to spin the arrow, at the most, at a time

Materials
- Chalk or large piece of paper; felt pen, card, pin

Procedure
1. Draw a rectangle 1.5 metres by 1.2 metres on the ground or on a large sheet of paper and divide into 30 cm x 30 cm squares.
2. Make a spinner, as shown, by cutting a circle of card (diameter 10 cm) and attaching an arrow with a pin to the centre of the circle. The arrow should spin freely.
   (Spinner should show L.A. (left arm), R.L. (right leg), R.A. (right arm) and L.L. (left leg)).

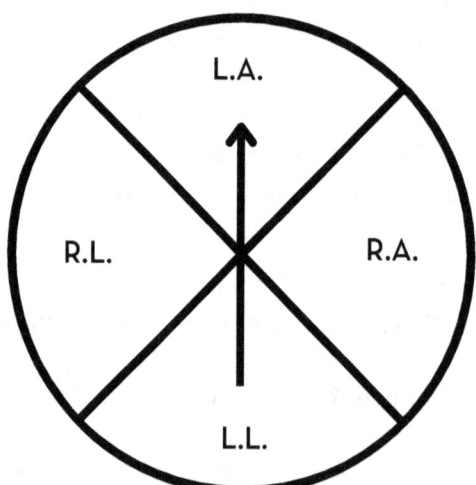

3. A spinner spins the arrow for each player. When the arrow stops it will indicate a leg or arm position. The player, beginning at the start position on the rectangle has to place that arm or leg in the appropriate square on the large rectangle.
4. The winner is the one who gets his/her body to the top of the rectangle.

Discussion

- After the game each person discusses their feelings as they got closer to the top of the rectangle.
- Describe the different feelings you would have if the game was played with a person:
  - You disliked
  - You did not know
  - You did like.
- Discuss the feelings you experience:
  - Standing close to other people (at football)
  - Standing away from people (waiting for the bus)
  - Talk about personal space. Measure your own. Walk up to someone you don't know, slowly, and notice the distance where you become uncomfortable. This is your personal space. Does it change with different people?
  - What difference does the sex of the other person make to your personal space?
- Go to an airport or bus station. Observe where people sit as they come into the terminal. Do they choose a place by themselves or sit next to someone? Discuss the possible reasons. Recall your own behaviour.

41
Signal Detection

Focus
Body contact and feelings

Time
30 minutes: four players and a person to spin the arrow at the most, at a time

Procedure
1. Find a partner, and a space by yourselves. One is A, the other B. Each pair works out an animal noise which they can both make, and agree upon (e.q., chicken, pig, cow).
2. A's line up on one side of the room on hands and knees, and B's the other, but partners should not be opposite each other.
3. On the go signal, the A's close their eyes or are blindfolded, and attempt to find group B partners by crawling across the room following the noise, which group B's can make every three seconds. This is the only noise B's can make. No-one is allowed to speak.
4. Tell participants to move slowly and stop if they touch another person, before listening again and moving to their partner.

Variation
1. Everyone must slide across the square.
2. Both A and B close their eyes.
3. When A and B are lined up ready to go, and B's are blindfolded, A's change position again.

Discussion
- How does it feel to depend on one person for guidance, someone you can't see or touch? (e.g. aeroplane pilots). Does it feel better when you can touch or be touched by someone, or see someone giving you guidance?
- Write down a list of all the people that use 'touch' in their profession, e.g. doctor, teacher, veterinary surgeon, etc. How would it feel if you went to the doctor and they didn't touch you? Does their touch make you feel better or more comfortable?

- Discuss the situations where your mother or father touched you when you were a child, e.g. at feeding time, putting you in the cot, etc. Do they still touch you in the same way? Do you still touch them in the same way? If not, what is the difference? Discuss whether it is important to touch or be touched. What can you do about it?
- Find a friend. Sit in front of them and touch their face all over with your fingertips. How does it feel? Ask them how it feels. Then touch shoulders, arms, legs and feet. Talk about how you feel while this is happening and afterwards. Does the way you are touched make a difference?
- Role play and then discuss the different ways you use your hands and body when you:
    - Touch someone
    - Praise someone
    - Punch someone
    - Feel sorry for someone
    - Help someone
    - Hate someone
    - Love someone
    - Meet someone
    - Tell someone something, perhaps a secret for them alone.

42

Just Relax

Focus
Relaxation exercises to relieve tension

Time
20 minutes

Procedure
1. A person says the following: 'Lie or sit somewhere comfortably and become aware of your body. Become aware of tension in your body, adjust your position to become more comfortable.'
2. 'Become aware of your breathing; inhale slowly through your nose; exhale even more slowly; pause between each respiration.'
3. 'Become aware of your body; place your hands on your chest; breathe deeply, but slowly in and out; release all the tensions from your body. Let the tension disappear.'
4. Leader to go through all body parts (major) loosen each part, let the tension disappear. 'Continue inhaling and exhaling slowly through the nose.'
5. 'Become aware of the thoughts in your mind. Picture that they are written in a book; gently turn each page. Let the thoughts leave you.'
6. 'Your whole body is relaxed. Now be aware of this relaxation; concentrate on yourself; let yourself float. Go for a journey.' Let participants stay in this position for some minutes.
7. 'Now reposition your body back on the floor. Adjust yourself back into your body; make yourself comfortable. Slowly wake and sit up.' (This step to be done slowly, probably over a minute or two.)

Variation
1. Ice cubes melting. Ice melts from outside not just the head.
2. Puppet on string. Strings are attached to different parts of the body. Pull and cut the different strings. Can be played in pairs or groups.
3. In pairs: one lies on the floor and relaxes while the other tests for relaxation in their arms and legs.

Discussion
- What parts of your body do you find easy/hard to relax?
- What other activities do you do to relax? How do they help?

43

Murder

Focus
Eye contact, communication, and responsibility

Time
30 minutes

Procedure
1. Everyone sits in a circle and covers their eyes. The organiser chooses a murderer (unknown to the others) by tapping that person on the head.
2. Everyone uncovers their eyes and the murderer may kill anybody in the group by winking at them.
3. If a person receives a wink they must count to 5 and fall forward and say 'aaahh!' (He is dead and cannot participate in the rest of the game).
4. If a person spots another person winking at someone, they may accuse that person of being the murderer, by pointing at the accused, and saying, 'I think X is the murderer'.
5. After the accusation has been made, the accuser must have someone to back up their claim. If not, the accuser must withdraw from the game. The suspect does not have to say whether they are the murderer or not.
6. A murderer is dead if they are accused correctly by two people, and a new game starts.
7. If an accuser and a witness are wrong, they both must withdraw from the game.

Variation
1. The murderer may be chosen by the group, choosing a piece of paper from a box. The one who chooses the only piece of paper with an X on it, is the murderer.
2. Choose 2 murderers.

Discussion

- Find a partner. Talk to them about the weather for 1 minute. While you are doing this make a note of where you look, while they are talking. Make a note of where you see their eyes looking while they talk to you. Much of the time we don't look into people's eyes when we talk. Should we?
- When a person talks honestly and sincerely with you, what do they do with her eyes? Discuss what is meant by a 'con artist'. Can you give examples?
- How do you feel about accusing someone of something and then finding out they didn't do it? Give examples. Listen for people to say these statements:
    - 'They made me do it'
    - 'They did it, not me'
    - 'I didn't want to, but they said it would be OK.'
    - 'It's your fault'
    - 'If you hadn't done that, I would have been alright'
- Discuss the statements. What do they really say, or mean? Can someone else make you do something? What does 'You can lead a horse to water, but you can't make them drink' mean?

44
Finding Partners 1

Focus
Warm up activities

Time
35 minutes

Materials
- Sticky labels or pieces of paper and tape

Procedure
1. The group leader gives a song title secretly to each person, making sure that at least two people have the same title.
2. Everyone walks around the room, humming the tune, until they find someone humming the same tune.

Variation
1. The group leader sticks one of a pair of names, as a label, on the back of each person (masking tape or labels), e.g. Jack/Jill, King/Queen, Thelma/Louise, Rick/Morty.
2. Everyone walks around the room without talking until they find their partner.
3. Everyone sitting in a circle. The chosen person in the group turns to the person next to them and says:
   'My name is …
   and I am glad to be me because …'

   The next person introduces the first person to their partner, by saying:
   'Your name is …
   and you are glad to be you because …
   and my name is …
   and I am glad to be me because …'

   Repeat right around the circle, each person starting at the beginning and introducing the whole group to their partner.

45

Wring Out the Washing

Focus
Group communication warm up activity

Time
15 minutes

Procedure
In groups of 2 or more people. mime wringing out a large sheet. Allow it to drip, then unwind it carefully without dropping it.

Discussion
- What did you need to pay attention to, to communicate non-verbally?

46
Shut Up and Listen

Focus
Listening skills, summarising information

Time
30 minutes

Procedure
1. Make groups of three. Call the members A, B and C.
2. Person A talks to person B for one minute on a topic of their own choice.
3. After A has finished, B summarises what A has said. C acts like a judge, judging whether B says what A said, or not.
4. When this is finished, B talks, C listens and summarises, and A is the judge. The group keeps rotating in this way.

Variation
1. Talk for more than one minute, say two or three minutes.
2. A talks to B, but B doesn't say or do anything, just stares. Does this make it easier for A to talk? Discuss.
3. A talks to B for two minutes and B nods and asks questions to make sure they understand what has been said. Does this make it easier for A to talk and B to listen? Discuss.
4. What resolutions can you come up with to make variations 2 and 3 easier?

Discussion
- Write down a list of things that you watch out for to find out if someone is listening to you. How can you tell if they are not listening? Whose fault is it if they are not listening? What can you do to help people listen to you?
- Many arguments are caused because one person misunderstands another. Discuss some of the things you can do and say to make sure you understand what the other person has said, e.g.
'Would you repeat that please? I'm not quite sure what you said.'
'Is this what you are saying … ?'

47

I Am

Focus
Self awareness and responsibility

Time
30-45 minutes

Procedure
Complete these statements to the best of your ability.

Today, I learned _____
I felt _____
I would like to know _____
I wonder if _____
I wonder why _____
I wonder whether _____
I was surprised that I _____
I was pleased that I _____
I was displeased that I _____
I realised that I _____
I found it hard to believe that _____
I never knew _____
I plan to change _____
I feel sorry for _____
Love seems to me _____
I feel happy when people help me by _____
I wish the world would _____
To me, courage is _____
If you want to make me happy, try _____
I don't like the way I _____
I sometimes wonder about _____
I feel insecure when _____
I wish I could _____

Discussion
- Share and discuss your answers with a partner or in a small, supportive group.

48
Ideal Person

Focus
To realise that there are things you can change about yourself, and things you can't.

Time
45 minutes

Materials
- Large sheets of paper; pencils

Procedure
1. Divide into groups of 5.
2. Each group gets a big sheet of paper and one of the group lies down on their back on the paper. The group traces their image with a crayon.
3. The whole group then cuts out pictures from magazines of faces, hands, clothes, etc. and sticks them onto the outline.
4. The group then has to try and make a perfect person. Discuss what qualities the ideal person would have. When agreement has been reached on a quality, write the words chosen around the edge of the tracing (e.g. smart, tall, rich, strong, handsome, thin, intelligent, brainy, helpful, kind, pleasant).

Variation
1. Each person in the group makes their own perfect person.
2. After the tracing is done, the group writes on the outline all the things they would like to be.

Discussion
- Pin up the perfect person poster. Make a list of the words from the posters under these two headings.

Things that can't be changed	Things that can be changed
handsome	rich
tall	thin
...	...

- Discuss with the group how you could change yourself to come closer to being your perfect person. Find examples of how some people worry about trying to change the things that can't be changed (e.g. tall people stooping over; hair transplants, etc.) What help could you give them?
- Discuss individual differences in people. Work in pairs. Sit opposite a partner and write down a list of ways in which your partner is different from you. Don't forget things like ability to kick a ball, to run, to talk, to get along with people, etc. When you have finished, compare lists with your partner. If they have some qualities you like, tell them, and ask them how they got them, and if they would help you get them.
- Discuss some physical things which can affect the way people act at times, e.g.
    - Weather
    - Tiredness
    - Sickness.

  Give other examples.
- Is it helpful or a hinderance to think about a perfect or ideal person? Discuss: Nobody's perfect.

49
Life Line

Focus
To highlight significant events in people's lives, in a non-threatening way. To think about what the future holds

Time
30 minutes

Materials
- Ball of string/twine, packet of index cards, paper clips

Procedure
1. Each person has a long piece of heavy string or yarn, eight 7 x 12 cm index cards and paper clips.
2. Each member works alone.
3. Each string represents an individual's life. At one end is birth, at the other death. Using the index cards, make drawings showing the most important events in your life. Then pin the cards in order, onto the string.
4. Show your life line from birth to death to others. Give reasons why you drew particular cards, if you want to.

Discussion
- Form into groups of 6 or 8 and inspect each others' life line. Members may talk to the rest of the group about any part of their life line, but need not do so if they do not wish. The value of this exercise lies with the opportunity to display each life line as opposed to verbalising. Everyone has the opportunity to display what has been important to them and to consider future goals.

50
Heredity/Environment

Focus
Awareness of the way in which heredity and environment affect everyone's life

Time
45 minutes

Materials
- Piece of A4 paper each; pencils; ruler; a comb each

Procedure
1. Each person takes a piece of paper and rules a vertical line down the middle.
2. Rule a line across the top and make the two headings as shown.

inherited things	environmental things
colour of eyes	hair style
shape of nose	length of finger nails
...	temper

3. In the **inherited** column write down the things you have inherited from your parents and family. In the **environmental** column write down the things that you learn from your environment.

Discussion
- Form a group of four. Discuss your answers. How can you change the things in the inherited column? How can you change the things in the environmental column?
- Put a mark by the things you can't change.
- What can you do about those things?

Variation
1. Work in pairs. Look carefully at your partner for at least 2 minutes. Then with your partner's comb, comb their hair into a different style. Discuss how the hair style changes their features. Discuss any other differences you notice. Now let your partner comb your hair differently.

2. Work with a partner. Talk about the things you like and dislike about yourself. Don't go on to the next thing, until your partner has told you what they think about the things you like and dislike. Do you both always agree?
3. Work in pairs with someone you like. Observe your partner for some time, then tell each other what you like about each other. Keep going until there's nothing else to say.

Discussion
- Did you learn anything about yourself? Now ask your partner if there is anything they discovered as a result of the exercise. This could be discussed in the larger group and noted in personal journals.

51

Who Am I?

Focus
Verbal descriptions and self awareness

Time
30 minutes

Materials
- Sheets of A4 paper; pens

Procedure
1. Tear a piece of A4 paper into eight pieces. On each piece of paper write one word which describes you. Because no one else will see the slips of paper you should be as honest as possible. When you have completed this, arrange the papers in order, placing the one you are most pleased with at the top and the one you are least pleased with at the bottom.
2. What you now have is a wardrobe of descriptive words that you can try on, wear or discard. Consider one word at a time. Spend a little time considering how you feel about each of the adjectives you have written down. Do you like it? Do you want to keep it? Expand it? Discard it?
3. Imagine what kind of person you would be with one, two, three or all of these qualities removed. Reclaim the qualities one at a time. How do you feel now? How have you changed?
4. At the end of the exercise ask each person to record two things they have learned about themself. If there is time, share 'I learned ... ' statements.

Variation
1. Who am I, my favourite colour. Make a list of eight things that your favourite colour reminds you of. Put them in order of preference, with the ones you are most pleased with at the top. Look at the list and see if you want to discard or add favourite colour things. Write a poem, a verse about your favourite colour things.
2. Repeat the activity with your most disliked colour.

52
Coat of Arms

Focus
Building an environment of positive support. This exercise is a way of combining several self enhancing questions with some art work and small group disclosures.

Time
1 hour

Procedure
Print sheets with designs as shown and distribute them. Draw an individual coat of arms by making a drawing in each section from 1-7, to illustrate:

Section 1: The most significant event in your life from birth to age eleven.
Section 2: The most significant events in your life from age eleven to the present.
Section 3: Your greatest success or achievement in the past year.
Section 4: Your happiest moment in the past year.
Section 5: If you had one year to live and were guaranteed success in whatever you attempted, what would you try and do?
Section 6: Something you are good at.
Section 7: When you die, which three words would you most like other people to think about you?

Any number of questions could be substituted for those above in order to adapt the exercise to different age levels, e.g.
- What is something you are striving to become or be?
- What is your family's greatest achievement?
- What would you want to accomplish by the time you are sixty-five?
- Draw a picture of something you would like to become better at doing.

Discussion
- Form groups of 5 or 6 and share what you have done.

53
21 Questions

Focus
To highlight self awareness

Time
20 minutes answering the questions and 20 minutes discussing answers

Materials
- Question sheets (see below)

Procedure
1. At first each member works alone while answering the questions. Then divide into groups of about 6 to discuss answers. Hand out a sheet to each member with the following questions.

   Write answers to each of the following:
   1. What would you like to do, have, or accomplish?
   2. What do you wish would happen?
   3. What would you like to do better?
   4. What do you wish you had more time for? More money for?
   5. What more would you like to get out of life?
   6. What are your unfulfilled ambitions?
   7. What angered you recently?
   8. What makes you tense or anxious?
   9. What do you have complaints about?
   10. What misunderstandings have you had?
   11. With whom would you like to get along better?
   12. What changes, for the worse or for better, do you sense in the attitudes of others?
   13. What would you like to get others to do?
   14. What changes would you like to introduce?
   15. What takes too long?
   16. What are you wasting?
   17. What is too complicated?
   18. What blocks exist in your life?
   19. In what ways are you inefficient?
   20. What wears you out?
   21. What would you like to organise better?

2. Divide into groups to discuss your answers. Make 'I learned' statements, or discuss how the assignment made you feel. Record your answers in your journals.

Discussion
- What things did you become aware of, that influence your behaviour?
- If you can pinpoint the reasons for some of your behaviour, you may want to change aspects that you don't like. Goal-setting is a natural progression.
- Can you use it to make you life easier, or better?

54

Values

Focus
The goal of this exercise is to highlight that it is not sufficient to believe or to think you have a value, but rather that something is a value only if it is acted upon.

Time
45 minutes or longer

Materials
- Whiteboard and chairs set in a circle

Procedure
1. Brainstorm with the group some of the values they hold in various fields, e.g.
    - Manners – are they old fashioned?
    - Pride – are there things we still need to be proud of?
    - Clothes – how important are clothes at work? at play?
    - Behaviour on sports fields
    - Family life – are there any rules?
2. Write these on a whiteboard or large piece of paper.
3. Now, individually, choose two values you believe in and write down the last time you acted on those values and what you did.
4. Break into groups of 6 or 8. Discuss the values that you have fully acted on and say what you did. Do you always act in a way consistent with the values you hold? If not, why not?
5. The distinction between a belief, attitude, or a feeling about a value as opposed to acting on a value may be brought to light. Discuss 'value indicators' (i.e. those things you say are values, but which you don't necessarily act upon, say in a crisis).

55
My Bag of Skin

Focus
Getting to know more about your body

Time
10 minutes

Materials
- Quiet room with carpet; torch; paper; pencils and crayons.

Procedure
The leader says:

"Find a place by yourself on the floor; lie on your back not touching anyone else. Don't talk at all for the whole time. Just relax and listen to me, then do as I say. We are going to explore our heads.

Rub the top of your head, use your fingers; feel for bumps, soft parts, hard parts. Now run your fingers around your ears; feel for soft parts, hard parts, bumpy parts. Run your fingers around the channels in your ears; is it dry or wet, furry or shiny, hard or soft?

Now close your eyes – run your finger over your eye; feel the eyeball. Move your eyes to the left and right; feel the eyeball move. Is the eyelid soft or hard? Feel the eyelashes; are they long or short, curly or straight, soft or hard, will they bend?

Move to your eyebrows; rub your fingers along the eyebrows and back again. What do you notice; are they soft or hard, or springy, do they lie flat or stick up?

Move your fingertips down your nose; feel the sides, are they straight or bumpy? Is your nose bigger at the top or bottom? Is it hard or soft? Can you squash it flat? Is your nose fat, pointed, bumpy, or smooth? Put a finger underneath the nose; is it hard or soft? Breathe out through your nose; is the breath hot or cold? Breathe in; is it hot or cold? Do you like the warm air coming out, or the cold air going in?

Now trace your finger tips over your lips. Are they smooth or bumpy, soft or hard, warm or cold, cracked or smooth, wet or dry? Do both lips feel the same; how are they alike, how are they different? Close your mouth tight. Try and push your finger into your mouth. Slowly let your lips go loose and let the finger slide in. Is it warm or cold inside?

Now feel your chin; is it hard or soft? Run your fingers up each side of your face along the jaw bone; where does it stop? Open and close your mouth; can you feel the joints move?

Move your fingers down to your throat; rest them on the front; swallow. What happens? Make a noise in your throat; what does it feel like? Where does the noise come from? Can you hear the noise? Can you feel the noise?

Put your hands by your sides; close your eyes; relax all of your body; don't talk. Think about the things you did. What was the softest part of your head; the hardest; the coldest; the warmest? Did you find something out about your face or head you didn't know about before? Did you find something you liked or disliked?"

Variations and Discussion
1. Look in a mirror. Go over the things you did while looking at yourself in the mirror.
2. Draw your face on a piece of paper and underneath write something you know about yourself.
3. Discuss the warm, cold, hard, soft, wet, dry parts of your head. What other features are on your face that you can't feel with your fingers? Put your hands flat over you face, then smile, then frown. What differences did you notice?
4. Write a story as though you were a small finger, or an insect, travelling over your own head.
5. Draw a caricature of your face or someone else's.
6. Pin a piece of paper on the wall. Put your head between the torch light and the piece of paper and get someone to trace the shadow of your face (profile). Make a collage of all the faces in your group.
7. Discuss things that you would change about your face/head if you could, and say the reason.
8. Tell someone else in the group why you like their face.
9. Walk around in the yard and notice which part of someone else's face you notice first, second, then third. Is it the hair, teeth, eyes or something else?
10. Sit with a partner. Smile at them, then frown. Let them tell you the difference. Ask them which they prefer.

56
Timid Teens

Focus
Relationships and communication

Time
No set time.

Procedure
Have students read out the following scene.

SCENE: *Living room of a student's house. Father, a large boisterous man, is speaking loudly in the centre of the room. Mother is seated in an arm chair and eagerly listening to her husband. Student is immersed in a book.*

FATHER: You should have seen Freddie. He sure had himself a high time. Boy it was really something. It sure was the best convention ever. (*The door bell rings, father goes to door and opens it. Classmate Bob enters.*) Oh hello, Bob. Come on in.

BOB: Hello Mr Saunders. Hello Mrs Saunders.

MOTHER: Well hello Bob. How nice to see you.

FATHER: David, get your head out of that book. Your friend is here.

DAVID: Oh ... Hi.

MOTHER: Take your coat off Bob. Make yourself at home.

BOB: Thanks Mrs Saunders, but I can't stay. (*Addressing David*): I came to invite you to a party I'm having this Friday night.

MOTHER: Isn't that nice.

BOB: My parents said that we could use the recreation room. I'm getting some new records and some other fellows are coming.

DAVID: There's going to be girls there too?

FATHER: Why not? You're certainly old enough.

BOB: You don't have to bring anyone if you don't want to. Alice could ask someone for you.

86 People Interacting

MOTHER: That sounds wonderful. David will be there.

BOB: Great we'll expect you then.

DAVID: Well, I don't know if I'll be there. I'm not too good at dancing.

BOB: Oh, you don't have to be.

FATHER: There's nothing to it.

MOTHER: David Saunders, show some sense. How do you expect your dancing to improve?

DAVID: Uh, anyhow, I really have a lot of homework piling up on me and I should get at it on Friday.

MOTHER: Oh for goodness sake, you know very well you don't have any trouble getting your school work done. You can spare one evening surely.

BOB: Well, I really have to go now.

DAVID: I'll let you know, Bob.

BOB: Sure thing, I'll see you about it tomorrow. G'night all.

MOTHER: Really David, I don't understand you at all. Why don't you want to go to that party? You never seem to go anywhere or have any friends.

DAVID: When I do go, I'm miserable, that's why.

MOTHER: Whatever are you saying?

FATHER: What do your mean miserable? You ought to have loads of fun at parties. Laugh, kid around as everyone else does.

DAVID: You just don't understand.

MOTHER: David, you're just shy, just a little timid. It's nothing.

DAVID: It's *Nothing*! It's everything. I'm bad enough even in class, but at parties and places like that I'm an absolute failure. You may not think it's to be taken seriously, but I do. I am not going to another party to stand around like a goof. I'm staying home where I don't have to be embarrassed.

MOTHER: David, I want you to go to Bob's party. You'll see, you won't be embarrassed.

FATHER: All right, that's enough of this. Let's not make a mountain out of a molehill. David will be at the party.

DAVID: Oh no I won't!

FATHER: (*To Mother*) As I was saying, that was some convention.

Discussion
- Discuss David's problems.
- Did Mum or Dad have problems? What were they?
- How did the different people want to solve their problems?
    - David
    - Bob
    - Dad
    - Mum

  Is anybody right?

- How would you help:
    - David?
    - Mum?
    - Dad?

57
Collage

Focus
Self understanding and building esteem

Time
30 minutes

Materials
- Magazines, newspapers, and other sources of pictures, tape or glue, and sheet of paper to use as background for the collage

Procedure
1. Individuals may work alone, then in small groups of three or four.
2. Cut pictures from newspapers and magazines which represent situations, and people, who affect your feelings about yourself. First, find pictures that remind you of feeling good about yourself. Make a collage of the pictures.
3. Then meet in small groups to share your collage. In the small group, each individual can take turns describing the kinds of situations in their life which give them those feelings. Plan to do something soon which will make some of those good feelings occur now.
4. Next, make a collage of pictures that remind you of people and situations which make you feel less good about yourself.
5. Share these in your small group. Then pick out one thing you can do in the next couple of days to prevent one of those situations which cause you to feel less good about yourself from happening.
   E.g. 'I feel embarrassed when I don't get my maths assignment in on time. Tonight I will finish my assignment. Tomorrow I will feel good about myself instead of embarrassed.'

Discussion
- Talk about ways of overcoming embarrassing situations. Give examples. Work out in your examples, exactly who is embarrassed on those occasions.

58
Power of Comparison

Focus
Self-evaluation – self understanding

Time
45 minutes

Materials
- Paper; pencils

Procedure
1. Write down an incident that has happened to you, in which you felt you had more positive qualities than others involved.
   In the second column, list situations which you felt you had about the same amount of positive qualities.
   In the third column, list situations where you felt you had less of positive qualities than others.

More than Others	The Same as Others	Less than Others
_____	_____	_____
_____	_____	_____
_____	_____	_____

2. When you have completed your lists, consider each of these questions for each column:
   - What kinds of thoughts did you have in these situations?
   - What kinds of feelings?
   - What was similar among feelings?
   - How did you act?

Discussion
- When you have completed consideration of each column, discuss what contrasts you see in your thoughts, feelings and actions in situations from one column to another.
- What will you do about the differences?

59
Working for Approval

Focus

Self understanding and building esteem. Sometimes a need for approval improves the quality of our lives. Sometimes it gets in the way. This strategy examines the extent to which our need contributes or takes away from our sense of personal worth.

Time

45 minutes

Materials

- Paper; pencils

Procedure

1. Work individually. Then share in any variation of group size. Use paper and pencil.
2. List the things that you do so others will like you ... or so they will not dislike you. Then identify whom you are trying to please, and whether working for approval in this way is helpful for you or hurts your general wellbeing. E.g.

Things I do	To Please	Helps Me	Hurts Me
doing homework	teacher	yes	
clothes I wear	friends	yes	sometimes

Discussion

- Now pick one thing that you do for approval which you think is not helpful for you. How will you change that? Identify who will be pleased when you make this change. Who might not be pleased? In what way will you feel happier or more satisfied?

60
Life Plan

Focus
Self Awareness

Time
45 minutes

Materials
- Paper and pens

Procedure
1. Make a list of what you love to do in life; any 20 things you truly love to do. The list is not to be shared, so you can write anything. Code lists in various ways, if you want, i.e. B stands for going to the beach.
2. Now, put a $ sign next to every item which requires an expenditure of at least $3.00 every time you do it.
3. Write A or P indicating whether you prefer to do each item alone or with people.
4. Put an R next to every item which has an element of risk to it, whether physical, emotional, or intellectual.
5. Place the number 5 next to any item which probably won't be on your list 5 years from now.
6. Use an * to show which items are your favourites.
7. Think of someone you love. Place an x in front of every item that you would hope would appear on their list, if they made a list of 20 things they love to do.
8. Date each item to indicate when you did it last.

Variation
1. Can be done several times a term.
2. After each entry, write 'I learned that I ...'
3. Write in journals.

61
Win Some/Lose Some

Focus

Self understanding; performance; acceptance of failure. Many of us need successes over and over again to let us know that we are worthwhile. We want a winning streak that never fails to keep us feeling OK.

Time

45 minutes

Materials

- Paper and pencil

Procedure

1. Work alone for 10–15 minutes, then form a discussion group of a few friends.
2. List some times when things have gone well for you, and about which you have good feelings.
3. After each situation on your list, describe what it was about that situation that was important to you. Then identify which situations had the greatest impact on you. Notice whether successes or failures generally have had the greatest influence on, or the power to affect, your mood.
4. Complete these sentences to convey what you think and feel about winning.
   Winning is ...
   Losing is ...

Variation

Write some statements that summarise your present point of view about winning or losing.

What have you learned about the kinds of things you choose to feel good about and the kinds of things you allow to upset you?

62
Good Feelings

Focus
Acceptance and self understanding

Time
45 minutes

Materials
- Pencil and paper (or journal)

Procedure
1. Work alone, in pairs, or in small groups.
2. Make a list of specific instances or kinds of situations where you felt completely comfortable and happy with yourself. Here are some examples:
   - Being hugged by someone who really likes you
   - Snuggled up on mother's lap when a small child
   - Soaking up sunshine on a fresh spring day
   - Exploring the bush
   - Stretched out comfortably on your bed
   - Skinny dipping
   - Being rocked and soothed once when you were hurt
   - Being with people in a situation where you know that whatever you say or do is OK
   - Sharing with someone whom you feel you have a great connection and understanding with.

Discussion
- When you have finished your list, talk about some of these situations with a partner. Then examine the list with your partner to identify what both of your situations have in common.
- In what kinds of situations do you feel satisfied and comfortable with yourself, and for what reasons? How often do you have these experiences?
- Identify which kinds of events or what kinds of qualities you would like to experience more often. Identify how you can fit some of them into your every day life.

63
Good, Bad and Ugly

Focus

Acceptance, self understanding and body awareness. The way we feel about our body may offer us a lot of information about how we feel about ourselves generally. This exercise provides an overview of feelings we have towards our own bodies.

Time

45 minutes

Materials

- Pencil and paper, or a duplicated drawing of a human

Procedure

1. Get individuals to draw a basic outline of a human, or give everyone a duplicated drawing.
2. Each individual in the group takes a turn calling out some part of the body. Then all members of the group will colour that part of their own drawing. Colour the identified part of the body with the colour that matches your response to that part of your own body. One possible colour code to use is:
   - Grey – don't like it
   - Black – don't know that part of me
   - Green – want to change or develop this part of me
   - Blue – I feel sad about or sorry about this part
   - Yellow – very healthy part of my body
   - Red – very happy and pleased about this part
   - Brown – uncertain

Discussion

- Discuss your drawings and the colour code system in a small group. Explain why you coloured some parts of the body in the way that you did.
- Identify each part of your body that works well for you. Identify what parts of your body give you the most pleasure, satisfaction, or are most productive.
- Summarise by completing: I learned ..., I want ..., My body ....

64
My Book

Focus
Self disclosure sharing

Time
1 hour

Materials
- Sheets of paper, stapled to make a book of around 8–10 pages

Procedure
1. Prepare the cover, and call it 'My Book', by ...
   This could be completed as a daily session for a week.
2. Title each page:
   1. My Statistics ... height, weight, shoe size, colour of hair, etc.
   2. My Family Tree
   3. My Friends
   4. My Favourite Places
   5. My Favourite Page ... animals, celebrities, seasons, artists, bands.
   6. My Poem and a Story About Me
   7. My Thoughts On ... justice, war, beauty, truth, courage, school, friends, etc.
   8. The Usual Day in the Life of Me

Discussion
- Form groups of three or four and discuss and share your books. You may need a few sessions for each person to complete their presentation and to continue discussions.

65
I'll Bet You Can't Use

Focus
Practice in divergent or lateral thinking

Time
20 minutes

Procedure
1. Choose one person to stand up and announce what they plan to build/make. E.g. 'I'm going to build a wagon.'
2. Other people can challenge this person by saying 'I'll bet you can't use ...', and name 2 objects (preferably objects or items that would not be associated with building whatever the person is planning to build!) E.g. 'I'll bet you can't use a propeller and a safety pin.'
3. To the person standing say: 'You must now say how you would use one of the 2 objects named by the challenger.' The game goes on in this fashion (usually becoming more hilarious as it goes on) with the challengers trying to stump the person, and the person being tested by trying to meet the challenges. When the person cannot think of a way to use one of 2 objects named they are out and the successful challenger takes their place, and announces what they are going to make.

Discussion
- Discuss 'lateral thinking'.

66

Robots

Focus
To experience blind obedience to commands

Time
20 minutes

Materials
- 6 chairs

Procedure
1. Form groups of four. Nominate two people to be called A and two called B. Place 6 chairs anywhere in the space.
2. On command, B's walk anywhere in the space and A's position themselves behind a chair.
3. On the command 'stop', all the 'B' robots stop and each controller 'A' begins giving directions to their respective robots in order to get them sitting on the seat immediately in front of them.
4. The winning team is the one in which the controller gets their robot sitting in the chair in front of them, first.
5. A and B change roles. B's become robots.

Discussion
- How were you feeling when you had to do exactly as you were told, even though you knew it wasn't the correct command? How did you feel about the person giving orders? How did you feel about the robots?
- Imagine you gave everyone in the room an 'obey orders' pill. What would you get them to do?
- Walk around the room like robots, stiff-legged, walking into each other. What is it like?
- Carry on a conversation with a partner robot in a robot voice. What happened? Was it interesting?
- Build a giant robot machine, starting with one person in the middle. Make them carry out an action and make a noise, e.g. They can bend over at the waist, move their left arm like a steam engine, and make the noise, 'boof, beep, boof'. Keep in time. Join the next person onto them, with another action and another noise. Keep going until the whole group is part of the Robot Machine.

67
Classified Ads

Focus
Classifying your values

Time
45 minutes

Materials
- Writing materials

Procedure
1. Find out what a classified advertisement is.
2. The less words used in a classified advertisement, the more money saved.
3. The price per word is 10 cents. Each person has $3 to spend on the advertisement. This means they can only use 30 words.
4. Everyone then makes a vacant advertisement for a suggested situation, e.g.
   - For a suitable teacher
   - For a good best friend
   - For a pleasant travelling companion
   - For someone to go to the beach
   - For a good parent
5. Write a letter answering one of the advertisements above.
6. Interview someone who thinks they can fulfil the requirements for one of the advertisements.

Discussion
- Compare the answers to the advertisements. Discuss the reasons that different people wanted different kinds of teachers or friends, or travelling companions.

Variation
1. On one side of a piece of paper write down the things you are good at, and on the other side write down the things you would like to do well. Find a partner, sit together, and change papers. Talk about:
   - Whether your partner agrees about the things you do well

- Whether they think you can already do some of the things you want to do.
- How you can get to do the things you want to do.
2. Find a partner. On a piece of paper write down the things you think are good about your partner. When you have both finished, exchange papers and tell your partner why you wrote those things about them. How did you feel about hearing some good things about yourself? How did you feel about the person who told you?

68
Palm Trees, Elephants

Focus
Creative thinking

Time
30 minutes

Procedure
1. Make a circle, facing into it. Demonstrate how animals, palm trees and clouds are role played, using three people, in the following way:
   - *Palm tree*: 1 person is the tree with two arms held up; 2 people form the branches by placing one arm around the trunk of the tree and holding out one arm.
   - *Elephant*: middle person forms trunk by bending over with hands together and held out; two people place an arm around them and make their ears by placing outside arms in a circular position.
   - *Cloud*: middle person makes a circle above their head by joining hands together; side people interlock their circles.
2. Everyone practises the roles. Then choose a referee who points to one person and asks them to be a cloud, elephant or palm tree. The people on either side must help form the character. If the chosen person can't perform the activity, they become the referee.

Discussion
- Discuss working under pressure. What happens:
  - Physically?
  - Mentally?
- What things can you do to reduce stress?

69

Forced Choice

Focus
Self understanding

Time
30 minutes

Procedure
Each person is asked to write an answer to the following questions:

Are you:
1. More of a saver or a spender?
2. More of a loner or prefer to be in a group?
3. More like a rose or a daisy?
4. More like breakfast or tea?
5. More like summer or winter?
6. More like a teacher or a student?
7. More yes or no?
8. More like the country or the city?
9. More of a leader or a follower?
10. More physical or mental?
11. More like a bat or a ball?
12. More like an arguer or an agree-er?
13. More like a rock band or a string quartet?
14. More like a clothes line or a kite string?
15. More like a roller skate or a pogo stick?
16. More like a bubbling brook or a placid lake?
17. More like a falling star or a lighthouse?
18. More like a filing cabinet or a liquor cabinet?
19. More like a tortoise or a hare?
20. More like a stitch in time or better late than never?

After making these twenty decisions, see if you can write a description of the sort of person you might be.

Discussion
- Show your list to a partner. Ask them to say whether they agree with your choices, or not. Ask them to tell you why? Ask a few more people.

70
Feelings Bingo

Focus
Practice at expressing emotions

Time
Activity 1: 20 minutes
Activity 2: 45 minutes

Materials
- Pieces of card, felt pens

Procedure
Activity 1
Write in large letters on pieces of card, the names of feelings: love; pride; hate; disappointment, etc. (enough for each group). Cut the words into letters only, then divide all letters into equal sized bundles. Put people into groups and give them a bundle of letters. The group that puts the most feeling words together quickest, is the winner.

Activity 2
Each person contributes an article, and places it in a pile in the centre of the room. One person pulls out an article, and says: 'The owner of this article must ... (Suggest one action like those below)
- 'Stand up and say three nice things about themselves'
- 'Sing a song'
- 'Act out peeling an onion'
- 'Say three nice things about someone else'
- 'Impersonate: a policeman, a teacher, a dancer'.

If the person does what they are told, they are the one to pull out the next article, and can tell the next person what they have to do.

Discussion
- Which emotions are easier/harder for you to express?
- How could you learn to express some of those which you find hard?

71

Relaxation

Focus
Relaxation

Time
30 minutes

Procedure
1. Everyone is to get comfortable, either sitting in a chair, or lying on the floor with feet straight out, not crossed, and hands by sides.
2. Breathe quietly and slowly and relax, beginning with the toes and moving up to the head.
3. Then concentrate on only one part of the body at a time, e.g. lungs, fingers, heart beat, feet, chest, and relax each part in turn.
4. When you have relaxed all of your body, concentrate on all the individual sounds and noises you hear outside your body. Concentrate on one sound at a time. Try to imagine what is making the noise. Include the sky, the surroundings, the floor, the walls, the furniture, etc.
5. When you have finished with one sound, try the next.
6. Relax after a while. Then slowly stir yourself into sitting up. Sit quietly for a while.
7. If you find yourself getting tense at any time, try relaxing just where you are.

Discussion
- What are the differences in your body when you are in a normal state, and when you are relaxed?
- Is it easier to think when you are relaxed, or when you are excited? Why?

72

Wanted

Focus
Reviewing your own personal qualities

Time
40 minutes

Materials
- Pieces of card, felt pens

Procedure

Activity 1
Draw a 'Wanted' poster about yourself. Make your crime a humorous one of not serious consequence, e.g. 'for putting too much jam on a scone'.

Variation
Make a 'Job Wanted' poster.

Activity 2
Complete these statements:
I feel sad when …
I feel happy when …

Other emotions to try are excited, jealous, suspicious, tired, annoyed, mad, etc.

Activity 3
Look in a mirror. Talk to your twin, and say how they are different from you – physically, mentally, morally, socially etc.

Discussion
- How do we make the most of who we are?

73

Personality

Focus
Personality comparisons and importance

Time
45 minutes

Materials
- Paper and pens

Procedure
1. Write down the names of some TV or radio, or film personalities that you have seen or heard frequently.
2. Alongside their names, write down what you think the good, and not so good points of their TV, radio, or film personality are.
3. Compare your answers with someone who has chosen the same personality. Did you agree?
4. Write your name on a piece of paper. Write down alongside it what you think the good and bad points in your personality are. Compare your own and your commercial personalities.

Discussion
- Is there any part of your personality that you would like to change?
- Discuss with a partner how you could each effect a change in your personalities to make yourselves closer in line with your ideals and values.
- How is the word personality used differently when referring to a film star and to you?

74
Good Times

Focus
Reviewing life times

Time
30 minutes

Materials
- Paper and pens

Procedure
1. *For 5 minutes,* write out a list of the things that you did last school or work day, and last weekend. Put a tick by the things you liked doing. Count up the ticks. Did you have a better time at school/work or on the weekend?
2. *For 5 minutes*, write down the things you do each day, e.g. sleep, read, wash your face and hands, have a shower, eat etc. Work out how many hours you spend doing these things. Make a table or graph. Study it. Could you make better use of your time? Should you arrange things so that you do more work, or have more leisure?
3. What is stopping you? Write down your answers and discuss with a partner.
4. *For 2 minutes in a group*, discuss the following: Have you ever sat down and done nothing? It's very hard! Get one group to just sit with their hands on the table and do nothing. The other group then times to see how long it is before they do something such as move their eyes, move their fingers or their bodies.

Discussion
- Discuss whether it can be useful to do nothing?
- Are we doing something when we say we are doing nothing?

75
Every Mother Has One

Focus
Reviewing personal qualities

Time
45 minutes

Materials
- Copies of list (see below)

Procedure
Everyone is to have 2 copies of the list below. Put your name on both papers.
1. On one paper put a ring around six of the words that describe you best.

quiet	fighter	clumsy
slow	disobedient	good
religious	successful	helpful
obedient	optimistic	moody
loud	failure	angry
romantic	honest	jealous
practical	unhappy	careless
sparkling	sad	perfectionist
happy	friendly	different
smart	responsible	boring
energetic	co-operative	conscientious
peaceful	dreamer	impulsive
exciting	careful	dumb
sensitive	funny	sarcastic

2. Choose a partner. Give them the sheet not marked and ask them to put a ring around six adjectives that best describe you. Compare their and your choices. If there are differences, discuss why.
3. Choose groups of 3 or 4, and discuss each person's choices. Let them explain why they chose their words. Discuss whether you agree with the other choices. This is a time for sharing and listening, and not for judgement.

Discussion
- After the discussion with others, do you want to make any changes to your list? What would they be and how would they make a difference?

76
I'm OK

Focus
Recalling personal strengths

Time
30 minutes

Materials
- Paper/cards, pens

Procedure
1. In a large group discuss 'personal strengths'. Take it in turns to say one good thing about yourself, such as:
   - 'I'm good at cricket'
   - 'I'm strong'
   - 'I'm a hard worker'
   - 'I smile a lot'
   - 'I have a sense of humour'
2. Each person is to write their name on a piece of paper or card. Walk around the room and exchange cards with someone. Write down on them a 'strength' which you think the other person has. Exchange cards a number of times. In the group, read out what is written on your card.

Discussion
- Now write down on your own card what strengths you think you have, then those you would like to have.
- Discuss with the group how you might attain any one of those strengths.

77

Childhood Days

Focus

Relaxation practice and fantasy recall

Time

45 minutes

Procedure

1. Get everyone to lie on their backs on the floor with legs straight out and not touching, and feet loose. Arms by sides, not touching the body, with palms up. Eyes closed. The coma position may be more comfortable for some. Sitting comfortably in a chair will also work.
2. Get everyone to relax. Begin at the toes through to the head, and then reverse.
3. Suggest for them to think of a time when they were a child. Get them to recall where they were living. Recall going into the room, sitting on the bed. Recall details of the room – furniture; cupboards; toys; light fittings; doors; windows; curtains. Recall going to bed; getting up; going to the bathroom; having breakfast; going to school.
4. Bring them back to their own body, lying on the floor. Slowly arise.

Discussion

- Discuss what memories you recalled of your childhood. Were they pleasant? Or unpleasant?
- Discuss the importance of relaxation in today's hectic society.

78

Great Day

Focus
To be able to recall good feelings

Time
40 minutes

Procedure
1. Everyone is to find a place by themselves and then lie on the floor on their backs. Sitting in a chair will also work. Close your eyes. Begin relaxing from the toes, right up to the head. Breathe quietly.
2. Suggest that everyone think of a time when they did something really well. Where were they? What kind of a day was it? Was it inside or out? Who was there? Recall what you were wearing. Recall the excitement. Recall what the body felt like: arms, legs, heart, skin, stomach, muscles etc. Recall the mind effects: excitement, pride, wonder, etc.
3. Say to the group: 'I want you to recall all of those feelings of satisfaction and happiness next time you are trying to learn something.'
4. Say: 'In a moment I'm going to ask you to slowly sit up.'

Discussion
- Discuss what people were thinking during the relaxation.
- How does thinking help or hinder relaxation?

79

I Can

Focus
Reviewing your good qualities

Time
30 minutes

Materials
- Paper, magazines, coloured pens/pencils, stapler

Procedure
1. Make a book by stapling a few pages together. Decorate the front and back pages. Cut into a shape.
2. Start each page with: 'I can' or 'I would like to'. Complete the sentence with something you can do, or would like to do. Illustrate by drawing or cutting pictures from a magazine.
3. Show your book to someone else and let them read it. Read theirs. Discuss any different ideas.
4. Make arrangements to actually do one of the 'I would like to …' statements.

80
Good Feelings

Focus
Strengths, weaknesses and setting new goals

Time
45–60 minutes

Procedure
1. Everyone write down this list of activities. (See below.) Spend a few minutes adding to the list some activities that people in the group enjoy doing. Include things you do at home, inside and out, when you're away from home, at work, on a holiday etc.
2. When you have finished the list, go through and put a tick by the things you have done. Go through the list again and put two ticks by those things you do really well, or at a high standard.
Possible list:
   - Roller skating
   - Board skating
   - Board riding
   - Doing jobs for pocket money
   - Writing plays or poetry
   - Paint
   - Draw
   - Cook
   - Woodwork
   - Whittling
   - Taking photographs and printing them
   - Make a video
   - Go fishing
   - Go bike riding
   - Collecting cans, shells, bottles, stamps etc.

Discussion
- Discuss your list with a partner. Tell them how good you feel about these things.
- Go through the list again and put a * by those things that you haven't done well in, or those things that you would like to try. Make arrangements with someone in the group to try that activity.

81
Private

Focus
Public and private selves

Time
45 minutes

Procedure

Private

1. Write down the FIRST thing that comes into your mind, when you read these words, one at a time.
   - Religion
   - Politics and personalities
   - Education
   - Drinking and smoking
   - Sexism
   - Sex
   - Beauty
   - Parents
2. What is your favourite:
   - Drink
   - Music
   - Book
   - Movie
   - Clothing
   - Type of house
   - Social gathering
   - Spare time activity
3. What are the:
   - Best parts of my school work
   - Worst parts of my school work
   - Most boring parts
   - Parts I could do better
   - My special abilities
   - My ambitions
   - My favourite rewards for good work
   - My feelings about the people I work with

114 People Interacting

4. When you have finished all the lists, look through your answers. Can you find something interesting about yourself? Show your list to someone else. Can they discover anything about you?

Myself

Sit by yourself and answer these questions.
- Do I like myself?
- What feelings do I keep to myself?
- Do other people like me?
- How do other people find me?
- What makes me depressed?
- What makes me happy?
- What hurts my feelings?
- What makes me proud?
- Do I like my:
  - Hair
  - Teeth
  - Body
  - Chest
  - Feet
  - Arms
  - Face
  - Hands
  - Legs
  - Hips?
- Do I sleep well?
- Am I ill a lot?
- Do I make a special effort to be fit?
- What would I like to look like?

Discussion
- Discuss any of these with the group, or a special partner. Share as much or as little as you wish.

People Interacting 115

82

Paint Pot

Focus
a. Learning how to give and to receive compliments
b. Confidence building

Time
30 minutes

Procedure
1. Form an inner and outer circle both circles facing one another, leaving a pathway wide enough for a person to crawl through and between the circles.
2. Choose a person to be 'painted' with compliments.
3. Everyone in the two circles are to think about a compliment to pay to this person. When everyone has decided on a compliment, the person selected is to get down on all fours and crawl slowly on hands and knees between the circle, while the people in the circle rub their hand on their back while 'painting' them with their compliment, by saying their compliment loud enough for them, and the others in the circle, to hear.
4. Compliments should be positive, and exclude pseudo positive compliments, like 'I like your nose, it's the only nice thing on your face.'

Discussion
- Discuss after every 'painting'
    - How the selected person feels
    - How the 'painter' feels.
- Discuss the giving and receiving of compliments.

83
One Special Thing

Focus

To build a sense of group rapport through an environment, for self-disclosure and trust

Time

30 minutes

Procedure

1. Divide into pairs, A and B.
2. Carry on a normal conversation for three minutes, each person telling the other as much as possible about themselves. Pick things about yourself that you think are important to share.
3. After three minutes, come back together again as one large group in a circle. 'A' should introduce their partner by stating their partner's name and one thing that struck them as most important about that person. Repeat the activity, with 'B' introducing 'A'.

Discussion

- Talk about what it was like to talk to the other person, and what it was like to be talked about in the group.

84

Coopers Creek

Focus

To enable the group to consider the positive qualities and positive characteristics of people

Time

45 minutes

Materials
- Paper and pen; map of South Australia showing Coopers Creek (one copy each)

Procedure
1. Imagine that you have been asked to select five people to go with you to set up a small hospital at Coopers Creek, South Australia. Think carefully about the characteristics, relating to interests and skills, including type of employment, that you would want in the people you would select.
2. List the occupations of the five people you would like to take with you.

Discussion
- Discuss your requirements with a group.
- After this discussion would you change the composition of your group? Why?

85
Best Friend

Focus
How well do you have to know a person before they're considered your friend?

Time
30 minutes

Materials
- Whiteboard or SMART board

Procedure
1. Form a pair, A and B, who are good friends.
2. A goes out of the room.
3. B answers the questions below about A. Write the questions and answers on the whiteboard or SMART board so that the rest of the group can see them.
   What is your friend's:
   - Birthday
   - Favourite food
   - Favourite sport
   - Favourite hobby
   - Favourite subject, etc.
   (Up to 10 questions).
4. Bring A back into the room and turn them around so they can't see the blackboard answers.
5. Ask A the same questions and see if the answers are the same as B.
6. Change.

Discussion
- How well do you know your best friends? Your mother, your father, your sister or brother? Could you answer these questions for these people? Could they answer for you?
- If you could answer these questions, does that make you a good friend? Can you answer these questions about a Pop Star?

Variation

Make a separate list of the things that you and your best friend do together. Compare lists. Are they the same?

Make a list of the good and bad things about your best friend. Sit together and tell each other about your lists. Tell your friend the things that they do that upsets or annoys you. Ask them to tell you about the things that you do to annoy or upset them. Say what, if anything, you are going to do about them. When you have finished, say whether you feel closer to your friend or further apart.

Make a list of the qualities you would like to see in a friend. Check the list to see if you have these qualities.

Make a list of the things which cause you to have a conflict with someone else, e.g. washing the dishes, or the car; choosing clothes; your friends doing something that you don't want to. How can you overcome these conflicts, or must there always be a conflict?

86
Secret Messages

Focus
To be aware of others and engage in a listening activity

Time
20–30 minutes

Materials
- Paper and pen

Procedure
1. Sit in a circle in groups of 10–12.
2. A person in the group whispers a one-sentence message into the ear of the person sitting next to them. (Cover mouth with hand when speaking message). The message is passed around.
3. Each person writes down the message they passed on.
4. The first and last persons to receive the message, read aloud their messages to the group.

Discussion
- How does the last message differ from the first message?
- Although different, do they mean the same thing?
- Discuss in a group what factors might contribute to misunderstanding what other people say. (Misconceptions).
- What can you do to overcome the problem of message misinterpretations?
- How can you make sure no-one ever misinterprets your messages?

87
Trusting

Focus
Learning to trust other people

Time
10 minutes for each activity

Procedure
Six people form a fairly tight circle. One person stands in the middle of the circle and slowly leans while keeping their feet still, their body stiff, their hands by sides, and with eyes open or closed. The others in the circle gently move them from person to person around the circle.

Discussion
- Was it difficult to remain with feet together while being passed around?
- How did you feel passing the person around? How did you decide where to put your hands? Were you afraid you may drop them or were you confident in your actions? Why?
- What are the main ingredients for trust between people?

88
Artists and Blobs

Focus
Giving physical expression to emotions

Time
10 minutes

Procedure
1. Form pairs. One is the artist, one is the blob of raw material.
2. The artist forms their partner into a famous or infamous character or statue. The blob relaxes as much as possible until the statue is formed. When the artists are finished, they move amongst the statues to try and identify the character. At the changeover signal, the artists in turn reveal the name of their artwork.

Discussion
- What physical qualities did you use to convey emotions and personality?
- What parts of the statue did you use to identify the character?

89

Charades

Focus
To explore non-verbal communication awareness

Time
45 minutes

Materials
- Paper, pens

Procedure
1. Divide into 6 groups of equal numbers, for example 5. Three groups are letter teams A, B, C. Three groups are number teams 1, 2, 3.
2. Teams A and 1, B and 2, C and 3 will compete. Each team must select a timekeeper. Each set of competing teams select a topic, e.g. titles of plays, movies, books, etc.
3. Each team chooses 10 titles for opponents to guess. Write them on separate pieces of paper and fold in half, and place in a container.
4. A member of the letter team begins by selecting a card from the number team. They read the card to themselves and then attempt to communicate the title to their own team by non-verbal means only. Their team may ask questions and make verbal guesses. The timekeeper from the number team should time the charade and tell the contestant when the three minute time limit has elapsed. If the letter team guesses the title before the time is up, they receive one point. If they do not guess the title, the number team receives a point. The team with the highest score wins. Letter and number teams alternate.

Discussion
- What types of non-verbal clues were used most frequently in your group? Which clues were easiest to understand? Why?
- What effect did competition have on the game? On you? On your group? Was it fair?
- Are gestures substitutes for words, or do they reinforce words? Do you feel that people resort to gestures when they have a poor vocabulary?
- Why do you use gestures?

90
Build a Block

Focus
What we say is not necessarily what we mean!

Time
30 minutes

Materials
- Logic blocks or geometrical shapes

Procedure
1. Form groups of 3, A, B and an observer. A and B can sit on the floor back to back or on chairs with a screen between them. The observer makes sure that the team works according to instructions, e.g. no looking, no questions and leads the discussion.
2. A builds an arrangement of blocks (a pattern, 3 dimension, a large shape) behind the screen. A then gives only verbal directions to B, one piece at a time, as to how B should duplicate A's model.
3. A gives the building instructions while B can only listen and build according to the instructions from A. A and B must not observe each other's patterns until A has finished. When finished they can compare the buildings.

Variation
Let B acknowledge instructions and ask questions.

Discussion
- Discuss the difficulties of this activity. Did allowing B to ask questions make it easier? Approximately how many words of explanation were used?
- Did either A or B get annoyed? How did they show it or hide it? Why did they get annoyed? Did one person try to calm the angered person?
- Did either of the team give up the task as they found it too hard?
- Did any of the teams develop a quick system of giving directions? What was it?
- How can we improve both the giving of instructions and listening with attention?

91

Fox and Hare

Focus
To increase awareness of the senses of hearing, touching and seeing

Time
20 minutes

Materials
- Two or more blindfolds; a large room with some tables and chairs

Procedure
1. Clear a space in the middle of the room and group some tables and chairs in it so that they are touching.
2. Blindfold two people, one to be the fox and the other the hare. The rest of the group form the boundaries of the chase.
3. Spin the fox around while the hare hides among the tables and chairs.
4. The fox must catch the hare using their senses of hearing and touch. The hare must try to escape, also using these senses, but they must stay within touch of the tables and chairs.
5. Let others be the fox and the hare.

Discussion
- Share your experiences as either the fox, the hare or the observer.

92

Parent Tapes

Focus

To become aware of some of the things you have learnt from your parents and others, and use automatically

Time

1 hour

Procedure

1. Form groups of 4–6.
2. Each group are to choose one of the following topics or one of their own choice
   a. At home
   b. Travelling: walking, riding in the car or bus, in an aeroplane
   c. Having a meal at home or elsewhere
   d. At someone else's home
   e. At work or school.
3. Write down as many things as you can think of which you are allowed and not allowed to do, or are supposed to do, or not supposed to do in the situations described above, e.g. at home:
   - Wipe your feet before you come in.
   - Don't throw your clothes on the floor.
   - Do your homework before you watch television.
   - Don't leave the house until you tell mum.

   At the end of 20 minutes, groups come together and read out answers.

Discussion
- What are 'parent tapes'?
- Can you think of any situation where you don't have 'parent tapes'? Are 'parent tapes' useful? Could you do without them? What are the advantages and disadvantages? Do you give out 'parent tapes' to people?
- Write down the words which usually precede 'parent tapes' e.g. You should ..., I would if I were you ..., I would ..., Don't be so cheeky ... etc.
- Role play a scene between a child and a parent when the child has done something wrong, e.g. told a lie. Are the 'parent tapes' obvious? Try some more role plays, e.g. teacher and child, police officer and motorist.

93
Talking Without Words

Focus
Communication through symbols and signs

Time
4 sessions of ½ an hour each

Materials
- Magazines, newspapers, books, pamphlets

Procedure
1. Collect pictures from magazines, papers, books, etc. of symbols and signs used in our society: astrology symbols, industrial safety warnings, road signs, symbols from ancient mythology, religions etc.

Discuss these symbols and their meaning and significance.

2. Each group then chooses a subject and designs symbols for the various aspects of that subject, e.g. schools.

  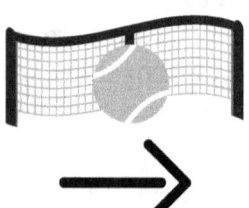

Hockey oval   No mobiles   Tennis nets this way

3. With school/parent permission, approach local industries or businesses and ask them if you could design safety or direction symbols for their organization.
4. Investigate the use of signs and symbols in other countries of the world, where they are used to overcome language barriers. Travel agencies and consulates could be sources of information.

Variation
1. Work in pairs.
2. Communicate to your partner how you feel sometimes, without using words, e.g. through mime, music.
   The list below might help:
   - Pleased
   - Happy
   - Frightened
   - Thirsty
   - Sad
   - Bored
   - Sleepy
   - Hot
   - Jealous
   - Cold
   - Proud
   - Hungry
   - Excited
   - Interested
   - Afraid
   - Sick

Discussion
- Discuss symbols and signs. What are their advantages and disadvantages?

94

Law of the Jungle

Focus
Sensory experiences

Time
45 minutes

Materials
- Chalk

Procedure
1. Move into 3 equal groups.
   Group A is a tribe of warriors.
   Group B are mountains and trees.
   Group C are people-eating plants.
2. Mark out a boundary of about 4 m x 3 m.
3. Make a starting and finishing point on the boundary (see diagram).
4. Group A: move to the starting point.
   Group B: take up positions as mountains and trees around the boundary.
   Group C: spread yourselves inside the boundary.
   As you are people-eating plants you can move your arms and bodies but not your feet once you have chosen your position.

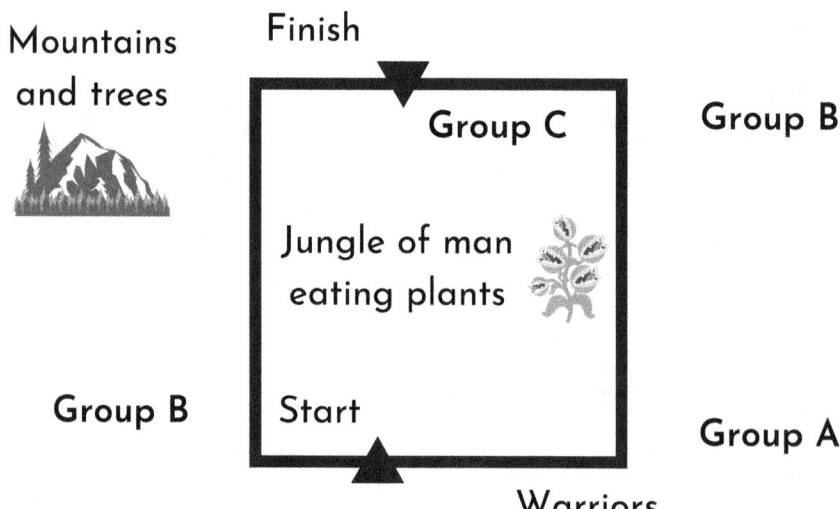

130   People Interacting

5. Group C: close your eyes. Group A: try to go from start to finish without being touched by anyone in Group C, or Group B.
   Note: Silence is essential.
6. Each group gets a point for each person finishing.
7. Group A must all attempt to go through the jungle within 4 minutes.

Variation
1. Change groups.
2. Change the time limit to 1 minute, 2 minutes.
3. Have Group C blindfolded.
4. Have Group C with eyes open.

Discussion
- Which group is it more fun to be in? Warriors, mountains and trees, or man-eating plants? Why? How did you feel when you touched someone and put them out?

Related Activity
Go on a blind walk. Take a blindfolded partner by the arm or elbow and lead them carefully around. Maybe down stairs, through gates, along pathways. Then change.

Discuss what it is like to be totally dependent on someone for your safety. How does it feel?

Discuss the word 'trust'. Is it important in this activity?

Discuss what it would be like to be blind. Would your other senses become sharper? Would you develop other senses to make up for your sight?

95
Observation

Focus
Observation of other people

Time
10 minutes

Procedure

Who is Changing the Movement?
1. Stand in a circle. One person stands in the middle with eyes their closed.
2. Teacher then non-verbally indicates to a person in the circle, who will be the be leader.
3. The leader will begin any movement (e.g. raising left leg). The rest of those in the circle will do the same movement. Tell the person in the middle to open their eyes.
4. The leader must change the movement frequently and the rest of the group must imitate. The person in the middle must try to find who is initiating the change. Once the leader is discovered, they change places with the person in the middle.

Get to Know a Hand
1. Sit in pairs and hold hands. Keep your eyes shut as it may help you become more aware of what your partner's hand feels like. Explore the unique features of your partner's hand. (3 minutes).
2. The leader says: 'When you feel you all 'know' your partner's hand, sit in a circle. I want someone with eyes shut, to pick your partner's hand from these three hands you can feel.' (Teacher picks 2 other students and partner).
Remember, keep your eyes shut all the time. When you feel ready, you must say which is your partner's hand.

Discussion
- Was it easy to pick your partner's hand? What features made it easy or difficult? What things did you notice about people's hands?

What is Changed?
1. Sit down in a circle. Look around at each other without speaking for about one minute.
2. Choose one person and say: 'Please leave the room and change something about your appearance'.
3. When this person comes back, the rest of you must see if you can spot what has changed.
   (I always ask people to use a complete sentence, using the person's name, e.g. 'Leanne, have you taken off a bracelet?')

Describe Someone
1. Sit down in a circle. Look around at each other without speaking for one minute.
2. Ask one person to leave the room. Explain the activity to this person, outside of the room.
3. The leader says: 'I want you to describe that person in detail'. (Clothes; colour of hair, eyes; any jewellery worn, etc.)
4. Ask the person to come back and check everybody's description.

Discussion
- Share what you have learnt about paying attention to detail.
- How are we often distracted?

96
Getting Acquainted

Focus

a. To provide opportunities to become acquainted with other members of the group.
b. To promote feedback and self-disclosure among participants regarding initial perceptions.

Time

35–40 minutes

Materials

- 12 blank sticky labels or strips of masking tape for each participant.
- A copy of the Labelling Category List for each participant. (See below.)
- Pencils or felt-tipped markers.

Procedure

1. The group leader distributes a copy of the Labelling Category List to each participant along with blank name tags. (You may make up your own list to suit your group.)
2. Each participant must copy each category on a separate blank name tag.
3. Participants mill around and choose a person who best fits each category. Stick a label onto clothing of the person you select and engage in a one-minute conversation. Then repeat. (12 minutes.)
4. The group leader forms groups of 5–7 members. Each group must discuss their reactions to being categorized and labelled (or not labelled) by others' first impressions (15 minutes). What is both positive and negative about first impression labelling?

Labelling Category List:
- Warm
- Intelligent
- Shy
- Fun loving
- Sexy
- Mysterious
- Sincere
- Happy
- Friendly

97
Don't Cry

Focus
How and why emotions are suppressed

Time
45 minutes

Materials
- Black or whiteboard; chalk or pens, or paper and pencils, rulers

Procedure
1. Sit in a circle.
2. Rule three columns on a blackboard or a large sheet of paper.

What is said	What is meant	What happens
• Be brave – Big boys don't cry • Don't be a sissy • Don't be a tom boy • Little girls don't get dirty		

3. Brainstorm as many of such phrases and sentences you hear being used on students; write them in Column 1.
4. Now discuss what people could really mean when they say those things and write them in Column 2.

1. What is said	2. What is meant
• Be brave – Big boys don't cry	• 'I get embarrassed' • 'I can't stand to see you cry' • 'What will other people think of me'

5. Now discuss what might happen when a person hears somebody saying one of these phrases from Column 1.

1. What is said	2. What is meant	3. What happens
• Be brave – Big boys don't cry	• What will people think of me if you cry?	• I'll stop crying because you're wild and you'll hit me • I'll go on crying because I don't care.

6. What do you think about this exercise? Was it useful? Will you make any changes to the way you talk to others?

Discussion
- What things could you say instead of the things in Column 1? Why do people (adults especially) try to make other people suppress their emotions? Or do they? Do the things in Column 1 help the situation?
- What about statements which try to make people cheer up? Discuss these:
    - 'Come on, don't cry.'
    - 'Come on, let's see you smile.'
    - 'Go away and don't come back until you're smiling.'
    - 'Stop crying and we'll go to the beach.'
    - 'Don't worry he's a pig, anyway.'
    - 'Come here and I'll kiss it better.'

  Do they solve the problem? Why do people say them?

98
Rumours

Focus

To improve the art of listening, by illustrating the lack of it to the group

Time

30 minutes

Materials

- An article of about 200 words for each group

Procedure

Divide into groups of six. An article of 200 words is given to a person in each group. They read the article and hand it back to the leader. They retell the story in the article to the next person in a whisper. Each person whispers the story to the next, until the last person, who writes it down.

Discussion

- The last version is compared with the original one. Work out where and why changes occurred in the story.

99

Focus

Focus
Practice in active listening and positive feedback

Time
1 hour

Procedure
1. Groups of 3 people take turns in the role play for 5 minutes each.
2. The 3 roles are:
   Speaker: who must talk about a problem, its side issues, how it may affect a person, a community or a nation. E.g, bullying, use of screen time, climate change, alcohol abuse, housing shortage.
   Listener: tries to understand the other's point of view. They may say, 'I think you are saying …' 'Do you mean?' to lead the speaker into clarifying the problem, but does not argue nor express their personal viewpoint.
   Observer: keeps time, watches the activity and how it takes place; not getting involved in the discussion.

Variation
The roles are changed and the game is run through with new players. Each feedback is timed for 5–10 minutes only.

Discussion
- The speaker discusses how they were helped or hindered by the listener.
- The listener tells the speaker what they liked about their ideas and the manner they were presented.
- The observer outlines what they saw and heard, discusses the process and what they liked about it.

100
Helpmate

Focus
Properties of a friend

Time
30 minutes

Procedure
1. Choose someone secretly without them knowing. (Choose someone with whom you don't usually associate). Concentrate on helping that person during the day. You might include them in your conversation, help them with their work, share your lunch, or get others to help them. Don't tell them what you've done, but write it down on a card.
2. At the end of the day everyone is to sit in a circle, and discuss the things that have happened during the day, and if they are aware they've been helped.
3. If your help hasn't been observed, show your card to the person you have helped.
4. Discuss why the person did or didn't know you helped them.

Variation
1. Write a radio or TV commercial about a friend, but don't mention your friend's name. Say what you like about your friend, and why others should like them. Present the commercial to the rest of the group. See if the group can recognise your friend from your advertisement.
2. Work with a partner with whom you don't usually work. Prepare an advertisement about a commercial product from a magazine. Choose three good things about the product and stress them. Make up a mock product out of boxes or cardboard, paper and paint and present your product to the group.

Discussion
- Discuss with your partner how you worked together! Was it easier as you got involved? Discuss the things you learnt about each other during your time working together.
- Form a large group and discuss whether the person knew you helped them, or not. Discuss whether it is appropriate to help people if they haven't asked for it. Can this be appropriate in any situation?

101
Film Stars

Focus
Thinking about your own aims and aspirations

Time
40 minutes

Procedure
1. Look through the newspapers or magazines at the entertainment advertisements.
2. Choose an advertisement that appeals to you. Then make a poster by drawing or photocopying the advertisement, however in the place of the names of the actors, put yours and your friends' names.
Show your poster to the rest of the group. Vote on which movie or play you'd go and see.

Discussion
- How does your poster reflect your own aspirations?

102
Clones

Focus
Using body parts to reflect emotion

Time
40 minutes

Materials
- Magazines, scissors, paste, paper

Procedure

A. *In Pairs*
   1. From magazines cut out photos of faces, eyes, noses, ears, hairstyles, bodies etc.
   2. Choose various cut-outs and paste them together to make a new person.
   3. Discuss and write down a name for your new character.

B. *Change Partners*
   1. Select a partner; one partner is to reflect an emotion in their face and body. The other partner has to guess which emotion is being acted.
   2. When you have each acted out a number of emotions, choose one or two, and re-act them. This time however, identify together which parts of the face and body are used to reflect the emotion: e.g. lips, cheeks, eyebrows, eyes, teeth, ears, forehead, nose.

Discussion
- What are some stereotypes linking physical action/posture to emotions? Did this show in the new character you constructed?
- What communication difficulties are caused by using stereotypes?

103
Autograph Book

Focus
Reviewing friendship values

Time
45 minutes

Materials
- Paper (small and large sheets), torch, felt pens, coloured pencils/crayons

Procedure

A. *Groups of Two*
   Make an autograph book. Have each person in the room write a small note saying something special to the person who owns the autograph book, and get them to sign it.

B. *Remember a Friend Book*
1. Get a few sheets of paper. Write the name of a friend on top. Write in a one line description of them, perhaps about the things they do or the habits they have, or their favourite things, or what kind of person they are. Pass the book on to someone else to write a comment.
2. At the end of the time, meet in a group, give the sheets to the person whose name is on the top. They should read out some of the comments.

C. *Silhouette*
   Pin a sheet of paper on the wall. Form pairs. One partner to stand in front of a torch, so that the shadow falls on the paper. The other partner to draw around the face and shadow. Colour in. Draw a speech balloon and make the shadow person say something funny, or serious, or factual, or philosophical.

Discussion
- Sometimes it's easier to write good things about people, rather than tell them. Do you agree? Why may this be so? Give examples if possible.

104
Friends

Focus
Reviewing friendship values

Time
30 minutes

Materials
- Paper and pens

Procedure

A. Form groups and have a discussion about friendship using the following questions.
   1. Do you have a great number of friends? acquaintances? Discuss the difference between the two terms.
   2. Do you have a best friend?
   3. How did you meet?
   4. Have you met a new friend recently? How did you meet?
   5. Have you found a good way to avoid arguments with your friends?
   6. Is it always a good idea to avoid arguments?

B. Write down his/her good qualities on a piece of paper. Now choose three of those qualities. Draw a line showing each quality on a scale of 1 to 10. Put a cross on the line to indicate to what extent you think your friend has these qualities.

kindness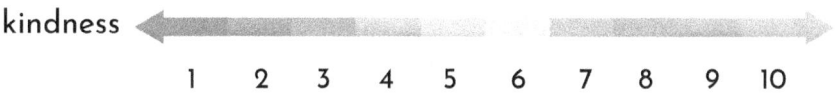

1   2   3   4   5   6   7   8   9   10

Now put a circle on the line showing how you rate on the same scale. Discuss your evaluation with your friend.

Discussion
- In what ways are your friends the same as, or different from you?
- Does friendship depend on being the same, being complementary, or something else?

105

Ghost Game

Focus
Using the senses

Time
45 minutes

Materials
- Large sheet, coloured paper/attribute blocks, music, wrapped parcel, paper, pens

Procedure

A. *Ghost Game*
   Choose a person to go out of the room. The rest sit on the floor in a circle. Choose one of the people inside the room to put a sheet over themselves. They can stand or walk in the centre of the circle. Call in the outside person. This person must guess who is under the sheet. After just looking, the outside person can ask the person under the sheet to give clues, e.g.
   - Whistle
   - Sing
   - Talk in a strange voice
   - Dance
   - Walk

B. *Musical Shapes*
   Cut out coloured shapes, or use attribute blocks. Pin them around the room in various places. Make sure there is one shape less than the number of people in the room. Play dance music. Everyone dances round the room to the music. When the music stops, everyone must attempt to put their hand on a shape. The one without a shape is out. Remove one shape, and play again.

C. *Mystery Parcel*
   Make up a mystery parcel with phrases like 'to the boy with the nicest smile' inside each wrapping. The parcel is passed around to music. When it stops, the one with the parcel unwraps the next layer, reads out the description written, and then gives it to the person in the group whom they think most meets that requirement.

D. *Initials*

Everyone writes their initials on a piece of paper. Mix the pieces up, and then hand them out again. The person who receives the initials must make a funny name out of the initials.

E.g. B. R. S. = Brown rubber sausage.

When you have finished, find the owner and hand the paper back to the owner. The owner must read out the initials, and the name: 'My initials are B. R. S. I am a brown rubber sausage.'

E. *Remember Me*

Choose a partner. Talk to your partner for about 2 minutes. One partner must then go out of the room. The leader then says to those who are left: 'Write down a description of the clothes your partner was wearing.' When they have finished, the other partner is called back into the room, and both people check the list for accuracy.

Play all of these games again.

106
Families and Friends

Focus
Reflections on your families and how they work

Time
30 minutes

Materials
- Paper, felt pens

Procedure
1. Draw a diagram similar to this one.

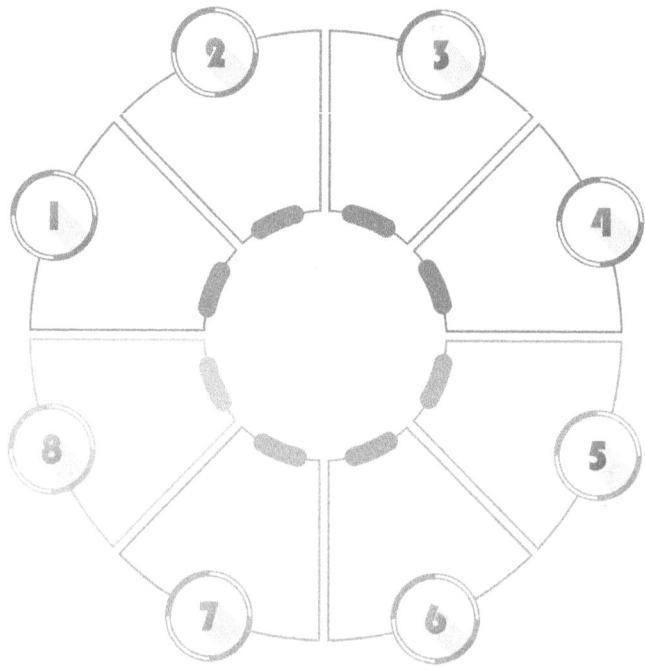

2. Write your name in the centre section. In the other circles (you may have to draw more) write the names of people who affect, or have affected, your life. The list will probably include mum, dad, some aunties and uncles, grandmothers and grandfathers, best friends, friends and even enemies. Write down in small writing what you have learnt from them, or how they have affected your life.

3. Now write down:
    - What you do for each of the people on the wheel.
    - The similarities between all of these people, if any.
    - The differences between these people.
    - Can you see any similarities between the people you like or dislike?

Discussion
- Discuss all of these things with a friend. Describe the people on the wheel, and tell your friend some interesting stories or anecdotes about these people.

107
Like and Dislike

Focus
Reviewing changes that can be made to alter opinions

Time
45 minutes

Procedure

A. *Like and dislike*
   1. Make a list of the people you really like and get on well with.
   2. Make a list of the people you don't like.
   3. Discuss:
      Is there anything you can do or change so that you like any of those people on your dislike list? Is there something that they could change to make you like them better? Write down alongside their names what you would like them to do, or to stop doing, so that you could like them better. Why don't you take the time to tell them how they affect you? Is it possible to like everybody?

B. *Choosing*
   1. If you had the choice of only one of these, which would you choose and why?
      - Your bed
      - The kitchen table
      - The television set
      - Electricity to your house
      - Water to your house
      - The car.

      Discuss your choice in a group. Did you change your mind after the discussion? Why? If yes, how did you change your mind?
   2. Put the items in order, the most important first.

Discussion
- Would the rest of your family put the items in the same order? Ask them.
- How do you decide whether you like a person or not? Can this change? Is it possible for you to like a person at one time, and dislike them at another?

148   People Interacting

108
Secret Agent

Focus
Memory improvement

Time
45 minutes

Materials
- Paper and pens

Procedure
1. Give everyone in the circle a number. Call out two numbers. Those people go to the centre of the circle, shake hands, and introduce themselves. Keep going for a few minutes.
2. Sit in a circle and test everyone to see how many people they can identify by name.
3. Find a quiet place in the room. Look around the room and write down the name of a person in the room. Alongside the name write down a habit that the person in question exhibits, but not one that may be extremely embarrassing, e.g.
Mary – coughs before speaking
Harry – giggles when spoken to.
Fill in between six to a dozen names. Read out some of your list to the group without disclosing the names on your list. Can others identify that person?

Discussion
- Talk about people's habits which you have noticed. Why do humans develop habits? Are they all harmful, or silly? What would happen if we didn't have habits? How can you change a habit?

109
Table Hunt

Focus
Sharpening the senses

Time
30 minutes

Materials
- Table, blindfolds

Procedure
1. Blindfold two people and place them at each end of a large table, with both hands placed on the table. One is the hunter and the other the prey. The hunter has to catch the prey by touching their hand. Each player must have at least one hand on the table at all times. No-one is allowed to speak. Then reverse roles. Time two minutes.
2. Two players sit opposite each other. The one blindfolded does not know who has been chosen as the partner and must identify the other person by touch only.
3. Two players sit opposite each other, the blindfolded one does not know who has been chosen as the partner and must to identify the other by feeling their hand, only.
4. Two players sit opposite each other, the blindfolded one does not know who has been chosen as the partner and must identify the other by their voice. The second partner must disguise their voice.

Discussion
- In a group, discuss the different clues that you used to identify someone while you were blindfolded, as opposed to when you were not.
- What can you do with this new information?

110
Me Cubed

Focus
Reviewing some values

Time
30 minutes

Materials
- Cardboard sheets, felt pens

Procedure
Make a 6 cm cube from cardboard.

On each outside face of the cube do the following:

Side 1: Draw a picture of yourself and complete the sentence:
My name is ...
Side 2: I was born in ...
and have lived at ...
I now live at ...
Side 3: My favourite animals are ...
Side 4: My favourite foods and drinks are ...
Side 5: I am reasonably good at ...
Draw it!
Side 6: When I grow up I would like to be a ...
Find a picture of what you would like to be, cut it out, and paste it on side 6.

Discussion
- The group is to walk around the room viewing the cubes. Each person to choose one or two interesting cubes, find the persons concerned, and talk to them about their cube and its interesting story.
- Hang a group of cubes in a mobile.

111
What's Your Name?

Focus
Assumptions we make about others

Time
20 minutes

Procedure
Make up groups of 4 and sit in a circle. No one is allowed to talk. After 2 minutes of no talking write down at least 3 questions you would like to ask the group, or any person in the group. Now, ask the questions.

Discussion
- When all questions have been asked, all groups form a circle and discuss the kinds of questions people asked. Is there any similarity? If we ask the same kind of questions as other people, why is this? What are the kinds of questions we ask people when we first meet them? Why? What could we do better?

112
Clichés

Focus
Recall of automatic reactions

Time
45 minutes

Materials
- Paper and pens

Procedure
In a group:
1. Write down as many clichés as you can. Change groups and write any new ones from your new group, e.g. 'Seen one, seen 'em all' 'There's always one bad apple in the barrel' 'A stitch in time saves nine'.
2. See if you can make up conversations using only clichés.
3. Go to a place where you can overhear other people's conversations. Make a note of the clichés people use.

Discussion
- Do you use clichés often? Discuss why clichés are used extensively, and whether they should be!

113
Journey With Friends

Focus
A co-operative venture

Time
2 hours

Materials
- Large sheet of paper; pencil

Procedure
1. A plan of a walk around the immediate area is drawn on a piece of paper. A large flat area is to be called a desert; stairs become cliffs or mountains; a drain becomes a river; playing equipment becomes a jungle etc.
2. Divide into four groups of five people, one group being the observation group. The observation group works out the instructions about accidents or incidents as in the example below. These instructions, given at any of the numbered spots, are to be role played for the whole journey.
3. All groups must note these points:
    - When going on the journey, no one is allowed to talk.
    - Each group must role play any incident or accident that the observation group gives them, e.g. if one member is told they have a broken leg, they must not use it at all.
    - All members of each group must start the journey together, and finish together.
    - At 4 or 5 points on the course, each group will be given instructions by the observation group.
    - Groups must finish the course as quickly as possible.

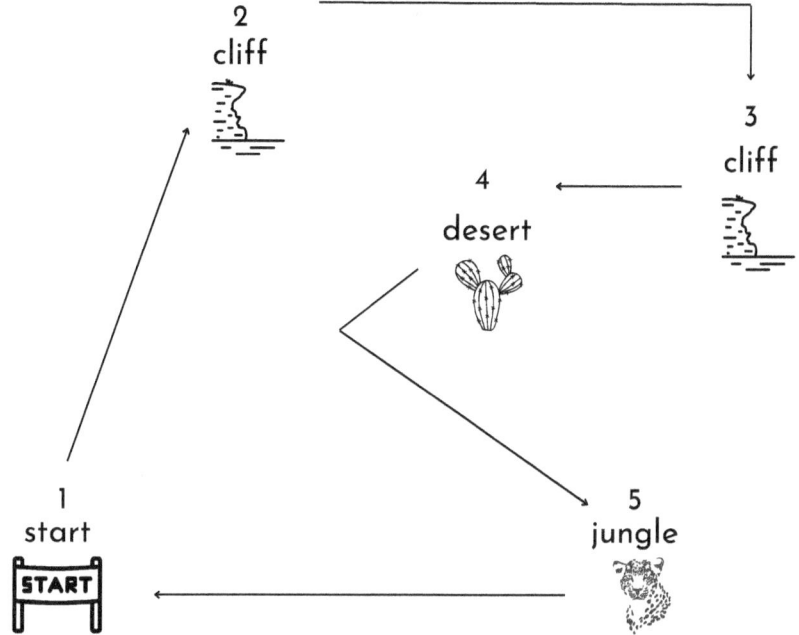

4. Group A starts first, followed in turn by the other groups. One person from the observation group will be stationed at points 1, 2, 3, 4 and 5, to tell the travellers, what kind of country they are entering, and to tell them of their accident or incident for this kind of country (e.g. 'You are now entering the desert, John, you become blind from a sand storm').
5. Only one person in the group is to be left intact. All the rest should have some accident, like a broken leg, arm, back, deafness, etc.

Discussion
- Talk about your feelings during the journey, e.g.
    - When you were blinded, or injured
    - If the group wanted to leave you
    - If someone tried to help you
    - When you told someone they were blinded or crippled
    - When you saw the group struggling along.
- Discuss this statement:
  'The person is more important than the task'. Give some examples of when you put the task before the person, e.g. 'Hurry up and finish! That's an easy job, you should have finished it a long while ago!' 'Here! Give it to me, I can fix it.' 'Go away, I'm busy!'
- Play the journey again, this time co-operating at all times.

114
Culture Game

Focus
To show misunderstandings that may occur between cultures

Time
1 ½ hours

Procedure
1. Have a discussion on what a culture is, and the importance and unimportance of customs. List points on a whiteboard or SMART board.
2. Divide into three groups, A, B and C. A and B find an area apart from each other and attempt to create the culture and customs of their own tribe by developing:
    - A basic language (gestures, etc.)
    - Type of greeting and farewell (touch or not)
    - Eating habits (utensils (type) or not)
    - A form of entertainment
    - Rules for individuals in tribes
3. Group C merely divides into 2 observation groups, and observes the preparations of groups A and B.
4. When a culture is developed, tribe A comes to tribe B's village for a meeting to discuss how they can live together.
5. Group C observes both groups in their preparation and in meeting, and makes notes.
    - Did they convert to known language and gestures?
    - What were the difficulties in communication?
    - How did some of the customs develop, through need etc?
    - What were the difficulties in organising?

Variation
1. All groups prepare tribal customs and the 3 groups meet.
2. Change groups so that a different group observes.

Discussion
- People from different countries are sometimes called by nicknames. E.g. wogs, polacks, krauts, etc. What names have you heard or experienced? What is the reason for this? Discuss.
- Discuss what changes people from other countries have made to your community in terms of clothing, housing, food, transport, etc.
- Discuss the different customs between countries, e.g. Christmas, greetings, marriage. How did these develop differently? Why do we sometimes laugh at customs different from our own? What can we do to overcome prejudice?
- Discuss the similarity of languages and customs between countries.
- Find out how to say 'Hello, how are you?' in as many languages as possible.

115
Ingroups/Outsiders

Focus
How does it feel to be in a group, or out of it?

Time
30 minutes

Procedure
1. Form groups of six.
2. Have an observer or two.
3. One group of six is the 'ingroup'.
4. The other group, or all others, are the 'outsiders'.

Rules for 'Ingroupers' to Follow:
1. When you talk about the 'outsiders' and to them, always use put-down words appropriate to the chosen role play as below, e.g. useless, one-eyed, bully.
2. Make up your mind about something and don't ever listen to the outsiders' ideas.
3. Make sure that the outsiders don't ever get the idea that they can do anything or that they are worth anything.
4. Pick on the outsiders any time you want.
5. Make an outsider aware of every mistake they make.

Rules for 'Outsiders' to Follow:
1. Never speak to an ingrouper unless you are spoken to first.
2. Always call an ingrouper 'Mrs --', 'Mr --', 'Ms --', 'Miss --' or 'Sir --'.
3. Always move respectfully out of the ingroupers way to let them pass.
4. Always speak quietly and obediently to an ingrouper.
5. Never join an ingroup unless you are invited.
6. If you are having a meal, wait for ingroupers to finish before you start.

The Game:
This is a role-play game. Using the groups you have split into and obeying all the rules for your role, act out any of the following situations:
- Going into town on a bus or train
- At a football match
- At school during recess or lunch-time

- At home watching TV
- Anywhere at all, having a discussion on a specific topic
- Any other situation you would like to make up.

Observers' Sheets:
1. What is happening to the outsiders?
2. How are they feeling? How do you know they are feeling like this? Are they all feeling and acting the same way? Be specific!
3. What is happening to the in-groupers?
4. How are they feeling? (Repeat question 2).

Discussion
- During the follow up discussion, steer people away from the sides they took during role play.
- Continue to ask how each person felt during the role play and if they now understand more about 'prejudice', 'hatred', and 'anger'. If outsiders felt bitter and angry, have them think about how people who have had years of prejudice would feel.
- Look at 'anger' and the ways in which angry people can cope with it when faced with seemingly immovable and unfair barriers (e.g. the rules of the game).
- Do you see any similarity between these rules and those that exist in society? Which ones? E.g. apartheid, sexism, racism etc.
- Can you see how apparently unfair practices and rules against minority groups continue to exist without ever being questioned? Why are they not questioned? What can you do about it?
- Who makes and keeps the rules of our society?
- What rules are there in your group situation which are not written down, but nonetheless are obeyed?

Note: A cooling-off or debriefing period must be allowed and everyone must be helped to understand that this was a learning game.

116
Inactive/Passive

Focus
Role play to practise assertive skills in a small group setting

Time
45–60 minutes

Procedure
In a group:
1. Form groups of 3 or 4.
2. Imagine you are in a situation where you wished to assert yourself and did not. Begin with a recent situation, one which will not cause too much anxiety and will have a chance of success in the role play, e.g. exchanging or returning faulty goods.
3. Role play the situation as it was. Then discuss the questions below, concerning assertiveness.
4. Now role play the situation asserting yourself where previously you acted passively. Have observers to offer feedback at the end of the role play, as well as people participating.

Discussion
- Clarify the situation and focus on the issue. What is your real goal?
- What would you usually do in such a situation?
- What might be stopping you from being assertive?
    - Irrational beliefs? If so, what are they?
    - Can I replace these with rational beliefs?
    - Have I been 'taught' to behave in ways which make it difficult for me to assert myself? How can I overcome this?
    - What are my rights in this situation?
    - Am I anxious about asserting myself? What techniques can I use to overcome this?
    - Do I have the information I need to be able to act assertively?
    - How can I let the other person know that I understand and hear them?
    - How can I let the other person know how I feel?
    - How can I tell them what I want?

117
Newspapers

Focus
To produce the first page of a group newspaper and notice the way people participate

Time
1 hour

Materials
- Newspapers, large sheets of paper, felt pens, scissors, radio

Procedure
1. Form groups of 4.
2. Collect the front pages of a few newspapers. Discuss in a group things like:
    - Headlines: how they are made up? where they are placed? how many?
    - Size, thickness
    - Kinds of articles on the front page
    - Other features on the front page, e.g. weather, television, breaking news
    - Pictures
    - Advertisements
    - Colour
    - Number of columns.
3. Get a large sheet of paper and felt pens and plan the front page of a newspaper. Use the current radio news as your information or make your own news.

Discussion
- Ask people to recall who did what in achieving the task. Who was most helpful? Why? Who was least helpful? Why? Did they know what to do?
- Find other reasons why they didn't help.
- In a large group discuss what the most helpful activities in achieving the task were.

118

Presentation

Focus

To use the creative and co-operative skills of a group to present information in an interesting way to others, and to give and receive feedback

Time

2 hours

Procedure

1. Form groups of no more than 6
2. Choose a topic from the following, or make up your own.
   - Prehistoric animals
   - Aboriginal Australians seeing and meeting the First Fleet
   - Road traffic rules
   - History of Australia
   - History of shipping, aviation, radio etc.
   - Problems of migrants in Australia
   - Hot air balloons.
3. Research one of the topics and write down about six facts which your group want to present to the others. Prepare a presentation involving at least 3 of the following. Make sure that all of your audience will be able to identify the six facts you present.

   Modes of presentation:
   - Puppet show music
   - Poetry cards
   - TV show radio show
   - Quiz play
   - Plasticine or other model
   - Seminar
   - A mobile
   - A picture
   - A collage
   - A talk

Discussion

- Large group discussion: give positive feedback to each group on their presentation.
- Discuss with the members of your group:
  - Who did the most work? How did that happen?
  - Who did the least work? How did that happen?
  - Who made most of the decisions? What were the decision-making processes?
  - Who 'gave the game away'? Why?
  - Who helped other people in the group? What did they do?
  - Did you have your say? If not, why not? What stopped you?
- Decide what changes you would make if you had to work with the same group again, or with a different group.
- Watch a TV program and afterwards discuss in a group how the program continually maintained your interest level.

119
Ostracising

Focus
To feel the effect of ostracising, or being ostracised and what can be done about it

Time
45 minutes

Procedure
1. Discuss the meaning of ostracising. Give examples. Discuss the fact that in the activity, someone will be ostracised as part of the activity. Note: Since this could be stressful to some, only volunteers will be chosen for the activity.
2. Mark 4 circles of 1 metre diameter around the corners of a square 3 m x 3 m.
3. Ask for four volunteers to sit inside each circle.
4. Provide a topic for discussion, or participants can choose one.
5. The idea of the activity is that while the group is discussing the problem, they must eventually ostracise someone, i.e. exclude them completely from the discussion. Don't listen to what they say and don't answer them. The group should not decide before, whom they are going to ostracise. It should just develop as the group goes along.
6. When it is obvious to the rest of the group who has been ostracised, the game stops and everyone discusses the activity. Debrief all participants.

Variation
1. *Musical Circle*
   Mark 4 circles at the corners of a large square. Everyone walks along the lines around the square, while the music is playing. When the music stops, anyone not in the circles is out and must walk away. Everyone boo's as they walk off.
2. Have 10–12 people walking around in a circle in the middle of the class circle. Gradually the group must exclude someone by forcing them gently out of the circle. They must not decide before who is to be ostracised nor must they discuss it. The activity must be done in silence. Have a discussion as before. Debrief all participants.

3. Have a group of 3 with hands joined. The 4th participant must try by any means to get into the group, e.g. asking, pleading, gently breaking the circle physically. Debrief participants.

Discussion
- Many people belong to clubs and associations because they all like the same activities. Every club or association has rules which the members agree to follow. Write down the name of a club to which you belong, and write down some rules which you have to obey. Do all club members conform?
- Discuss the rules you have to obey:
    - At school
    - At work
    - At home
    - In the street
    - At the movies
    - At someone else's house
- Discuss what happens to the people who break the rules. What can you do if you don't like a rule?

120
Building

Focus
Group interaction

Time
30 minutes

Procedure
1. Everyone stands in a large circle. One person starts off and stands in the middle of the circle in a comfortable freeze position.
2. In turn, each person attaches one part of themselves to the existing structure and freezes.
3. When the design has been completed let it stand for a while, then gradually break it down by participants slowly sinking to the floor, then rolling over and relaxing.
4. Now begin a new structure.

Discussion
- Discuss why some people join in quickly and why others wait. Tell the group of other situations where you perhaps tend to 'hang back', rather than pushing yourself forward. Discuss situations where you have little hesitancy in pushing forward.
- Discuss situations where you have seen:
   - People push forward
   - People hang back.
- Observe people who do not know one another, coming in to sit down on a bus or in an airport loungeroom.
- Try to work out why they sit where they do. Do they sit next to one another, or separately?
- What things encourage people to sit next to one another or separately? Can you design a room where people have to sit next to one another? What would you use a room like this for?

121
Apathy

Focus
To promote discussion about some possible ways of dealing with apathy and the feelings that apathy arouses

Time
30 minutes

Procedure
1. Choose two committees, A and B.
2. Decide on the same committee topic for both A and B. E.g.
   - A social to raise money
   - A fun day of activities
   - How to brighten up the organisation
   - A disco to get kids together.
3. Both committees go into separate rooms for 15 minutes to discuss what they are going to say at the combined meeting, but committee A is directed to be enthusiastic about the activity and committee B apathetic about the activity.
4. The committees A and B combine to discuss the activity, with A further promoting the activity and B being quite apathetic about the whole process and activity. The rest of the group observes.

Discussion
- What feelings were aroused by:
  - The enthusiastic committee?
  - The apathetic committee?
- Discuss what members of the enthusiastic group did to try and move the apathetic group. Did it fail? Why? Was it worth the trouble?
- What other things would it have been possible to do to arouse the apathetic committee?
- Reverse the roles of the groups. Repeat the discussion.

122
Co-operate

Focus

This game provides insight into our behaviour, whether we play to win or not. It shows the dynamics of co-operation with others

Time

45 minutes

Materials
- Large sheets of cardboard, scissors, felt pens, ruler, set square, envelopes

Preparation
1. Several groups of 5 members, each with a set of envelopes, may be watched by the remainder of the class who act as observers.
2. For each group prepare a set of squares of cardboard as per the diagram.
3. The lines should be drawn so that when cut out, all pieces marked the same will be of exactly the same size.
4. Cut each square as marked into smaller pieces to make the parts of the puzzle.

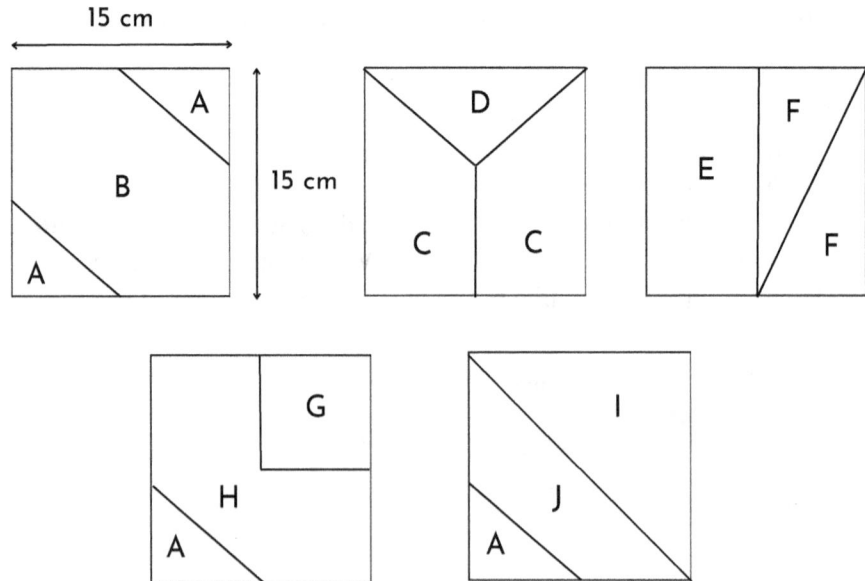

168   People Interacting

5. Mark the 5 envelopes 1, 2, 3, 4 and 5. Distribute the cardboard pieces in the five envelopes as follows:

   Envelope 1 has pieces   I, H, E.
                 2   A, A, A, C.
                 3   A, J.
                 4   D, F.
                 5   G, B, F, C.

6. Write the appropriate envelope number on the back of each piece. This will make it easy to return the pieces to the proper envelope for subsequent use when a group has completed the task.
7. For groups with more than five, have the groups decide which five will actually do the task, with the others acting as observers.

Procedure

Give the following instructions:

> 'Today we are going to do a puzzle. It will take five members of your group to do the puzzle. The others will sit outside as observers. Would the five working members please sit in a tight circle, and the observers please sit outside the circle. I will hand you an envelope that contains puzzle pieces. Take the puzzle pieces out of the envelope and set the envelope aside. Leave the pieces lying in front of you. Distributed among the five of you are puzzle pieces that will form five complete squares of equal dimensions one in front of each person. However, you must observe the following rules while assembling the squares:
> a. Each person must construct a square directly in front of them.
> b. You may not ask for a piece from any other member, this includes asking verbally or taking physically, as well as signalling, gesturing, motioning or in any other way trying to get a piece from the other members.
> c. The only way you can get a piece from another person is for them to give it to you.
> d. You may give any of the pieces you have to any other group member."

Observers must see that the players obey the rules. The winning group is the one that completes five squares first, and correctly.

Discussion

- What feelings did you have at different times during the activity?
- How did you feel when you could see the piece you needed in someone else's square? What did you think about that person?
- Talk about frustration. What other things raised the level of frustration?

123
Straw Game

Focus
Group interaction

Time
15 minutes for exercise, 10–15 minutes for discussion

Materials
- Large quantity of coloured drinking straws

Procedure
1. Appoint one observer to each group of 6 or 7 workers.
2. The workers sit together on the floor with a pile of straws in the centre.
3. The observer sits up higher on a chair or stool.
4. The workers are instructed to work as a group and to use the straws to make a big, beautiful design on the floor.
5. The observer keeps a check on how the group functions and writes down the following:
   - Who makes the first suggestion?
   - Who begins the task?
   - Is the first suggestion carried out?
   - Does the group start again? How many times?
   - Who does most work?
   - Does any one work alone? Does any one just watch?
   - Who talks most?
   - Is any one dissatisfied? Is any one destructive?
   - Are all the group members happy with the final result?

Variation
Use Lego or plasticene to make the design.

Discussion
- After completion of the design, each observer should report to the whole group everything that happened among the workers whom they observed (according to the checklist).
- The workers may then comment on their feelings while they worked. What did they enjoy? Did they feel frustrated? Annoyed? Satisfied?
- What helps a group to be productive?
- What are the pros and cons of working with a group?

124
Prepared Argument

Focus
Group interaction to discover methods of disagreeing

Time
45 minutes

Materials
- Paper and pens

Procedure
1. Divide the class into 2 groups, each with 2 judges.
2. The same controversial topic is given to both groups.
3. Some topics could be:
   a. We could not do without electricity for 3 nights.
   b. Millions would die if there was no oil.
   c. Insects will take over the earth very soon.
   d. Zero population growth.
4. The groups then go outside and prepare their arguments. One group takes the pro side, and one the con side.
5. They return. Each group sits in a line facing each other. They then put forward their arguments, someone taking a turn from each group.
6. At the end of 20 minutes, the arguments stop and the judges present their analyses of the group work in terms of:
   - Organisation of the group at the beginning
   - Who did how much talking?
   - Who used facts to support their argument?
   - Who didn't say much at all?
   - Did the whole group support each other? How?

Variation
1. Have only 3 speakers from each group, in turn.
2. The judge can decide if one side won the argument.

Discussion
- Are there different kinds of arguments? Give examples. Must all arguments be wild?

- Make a list of some of the words or phrases which can make an argument:
  - Heated (e.g. 'that's a stupid thing to say!')
  - Friendly (e.g. 'I agree with you, Fred, but do you think it is possible?')
- Make a list of all the ways you can think of to cause an argument, or make one worse, e.g. referring to a person's character, referring to a person's background, putting a person down or telling a secret about the person.
- Discuss this statement: 'A good argument deals with the facts, not personalities.' Give examples of arguments you have heard where someone has tried to win by verbally attacking the other person, rather than their argument.
- Write down a good reason why it might be important to win an argument and why it seems awful to lose (if it is). Discuss these reasons in a group. Explain what your feelings are when you lose an argument. Is it so important to win, and make the other person have those bad feelings? All the time?
- In an argument, sometime this week, say to the other person something like: 'I agree with you, you are right and I am wrong.' See if they smile, then check your own feelings to see if you are OK.

125
Today

Focus
Reviewing progress

Time
40 minutes

Procedure
At the end of a day or a session, individuals make notes, choose groups and then discuss:
- What you've achieved today
- What you've learned today
- What you'd like to learn more about
- How you feel about the day
- How you may have been able to improve your day/session.

126

Group Works

Focus
Review group procedures

Time
45 minutes

Materials
- Cards with questions, pens

Procedure
1. Form two circles, an inner, and an outer. The inner circle should contain only five or six people. The inner circle discusses a topic aloud. No-one in the outer circle is allowed to speak. The inner circle might discuss 'Let's organise a picnic' or 'should we have a fund raising disco' or a topic of their choice.
2. The people in the outer circle should have a piece of card with one of the following questions inscribed, and should write down the answer to the questions as the inner circle discuss their topic.
   a. Which people spoke?
   b. Who spoke the most?
   c. Who spoke the least?
   d. Who helped the group the most to find a solution?
   e. Who hindered the group? What did they do?
   f. How did people help each other?
   g. Who listened the best? How do you know?
   h. Was there a leader?
   i. Was there a time when someone could have helped but didn't?
   j. Who didn't listen well? How do you know?
   k. What was the changing point in the group? When did they start to reach a decision?
   l. What was the decision of the group?

Discussion
- Reform into a large circle, and discuss the questions and answers.
- Discuss how the people in the inner circle could have improved their performance.

127
Telegram Ti-Tree

Focus
Alternative ways of saying thanks

Time
20 minutes

Materials
- Tree branch, cards, string, pens

Procedure
Put the dead branch of a tree with plenty of twigs in a bucket filled with sand so that it stands straight. Use cards that can be attached to the tree with wool or string. Everyone is to create a card with a positive message for someone via writing or drawing. Then hang it on the tree.

Depending on your situation, it may be important to make sure every person receives a positive message. The activity could be done for individuals over many weeks.

Mary ... I like you

Sergi ... thank you for your help yesterday

Bill ... you are a good friend

Discussion
- Discuss the effect the Ti-tree had on the group.
- What other structures may help in giving compliments?

128

Smilo

Focus
Co-operation

Time
40 minutes

Materials
- Bucket of water, cup and teaspoons

Procedure

Smilo
Make up two teams of 6. Each team sits opposite each other. Team A tries to make Team B smile. Then change around.

Water Wheel
1. Choose four teams of up to six players per team. Form them as four spokes in a wheel.

2. Place a bucket of water at the hub of the wheel.
3. Each last player has a cup. Each leader has a teaspoon. On the signal 'Go' the leader must fill the teaspoon and pass it down the line. The last player must pour the water into the cup, and pass the spoon back. The team with the most water after five minutes wins.

Discussion
- Can co-operation exist without competition? If yes, give examples.

129
Finding Partners 2

Focus
To choose partners and discuss relative merits of different methods

Time
Between 2–10 minutes for each activity

Procedure

Names in a Box
Write each person's name on a piece of paper. Put all the papers in a box. Pull out pairs of names as partners.

Dog and Bone
1. Everyone sits in a circle. The leader gives each person in the circle a number, so that there are two people with the number 2, two people with the number 3, etc. until everyone has a number. For 30 people, everyone in the circle would have a number between 1 and 15. Put an article in the centre of the circle. When the leader calls out a number, the two people with that number race to see who can pick up the article and return to their place in the circle without being touched. Your partner is the one who has the same number as you.
2. Find a partner within the room who is about your size, height and weight. That person becomes your partner.
3. Choose someone who you would like to work with as your partner.
4. On a sheet of paper or cardboard, write down answers only to these questions:
   - What is your favourite food?
   - What is your favourite drink?
   - Where do you like to go for holidays?
   - What is your favourite colour?
   - What is your favourite TV program?
   - Who is your favourite film star?

   Hold this sheet in front of you and walk around the room. Find somebody whose interests are similar to yours. Ask them if they'd like to be your partner.

Discussion
- What are the problems in having partners designated?
- What are the advantages of choosing partners, over having them chosen for you?
- What would it be like to be
  - Always chosen first?
  - Always chosen last?

  in activities 3 and 4?
- Discuss ways in which you could choose the membership of larger groups. What are the advantages and disadvantages of each?

130
Co-operation

Focus
How you feel in a situation of 'no co-operation' and 'complete co-operation' with another person or persons

Time
55 minutes

Materials
- Sheet of paper, a pencil, set of coloured pencils for each pair, whiteboard, list of words

Procedure
Everyone in a circle on the carpet. Choose 2 people to sit in the middle of the circle. Explain that one person has IT (no definition to be given), and wants to keep IT, and the other person wants IT. Then say 'Go Ahead'.

Discussion
Discuss feelings of the person who
- Has IT
- Does not have IT

Discuss practical examples, e.g. brother and sister at home, in classroom borrowing a pencil, a book.

Discuss alternative methods of managing a problem between two people.

Variation
1. Give everyone a sheet of paper. Have only one pen, and one set of coloured pencils. Give students (in pairs) simple topics to write a one page project.
2. Art: Discuss a mural, e.g. street scene, forest scene, beach scene and work out how each pair of students can contribute to the class mural.

3. Group of 5/6. Each group is to have a piece of paper and a pencil (no leader to be elected). Organiser writes on the whiteboard or SMART board this list of camping materials:
   - Tent
   - Matches
   - 6 cans of baked beans
   - A kerosene light
   - A flashlight
   - A stove
   - A 4-litre container of water
   - 4 camp stretchers
   - 1½ kg of butter
   - A dozen eggs
   - 3 loaves of bread
   - 1 piece of canvas
   - 10 metres of rope
   - A fishing line.

   Explain that the group can only carry 6 things because they are going into heavy country (7 things if they don't take a tent). Each group must decide the 6 things they are going to take (time 20 minutes). Each group reads their list to the large group. Then, with the whole group, discuss reasons for various things (e.g. don't need fishing lines without bait). After a whole class discussion, go back to the group to see if the group wants to change their list.

Discussion
- Why do groups or people change their minds?
- How do they change their minds?
- Do people change their minds for reasons other than logical ones? (e.g. pride).
- How can we accommodate to each other's changes?

131
What Am I?

Focus
Co-operation in group problem solving

Time
20 minutes each activity

Materials
- Cardboard pieces, scissors, felt pens, paper, whiteboard, matches and glue

Procedure

Animal, Vegetable, Mineral or Plastic
1. One person in the group is to secretly choose an object that belongs in the group of either animal, vegetable, mineral or plastic, e.g. birthday card.
2. The others in the group are to ask questions to try and ascertain the name of the object. However, the first person may only answer YES or NO.
3. Only 20 questions allowed, e.g.
   - Is it animal? NO
   - Is it vegetable? YES
   - Is it used in the home? YES
   - Is it used in the kitchen? YES
   - Is it used in cookery? NO

Name Scrabble
1. Form groups of six
2. Each person to write the letters of their first name on the same sized piece of card. Cut out the letters individually and place them all in a box. Place in the box other letters of the alphabet as well.
3. Each person to take out seven pieces. Place any names that can be made up from the pieces on the table and take out that number of pieces from the box. Take turns. If unable to make up a name on your turn, take a letter from the box. The person who makes up the most names is the winner. Pieces can be exchanged with partners instead of taking from the box.

What's in a Name?
1. Form groups of six. Each person in turn writes their first name on paper, or a whiteboard or SMART board.
2. The group must then use the letters of the name to describe that person, e.g.
    - Terrific
    - OK
    - Neat
    - Young
3. Take turns.

Charades
1. Form groups of six.
2. Write down the names of six objects that anyone in the group can mime. A person from each group takes a turn to charade an object from their list. A group gets a point for every other group that discovers their charade within two minutes.

Match Castle
1. Form groups of six.
2. Give each group a box of matches, and glue. The winning group is the one that can build the highest self supporting building within five minutes.
3. To be successful, the building must be recognizable, e.g. a castle, Eiffel Tower, etc.

Discussion
- Which groups worked the best together? Why? What helped?
- Discuss group co-operation. Play one activity again with the aim of getting the best co-operation possible in your group. What were the differences in the first round of games?
- Discuss the rules of 'co-operation'.

132
Role Plays

Focus
Conflict, problem solving, and negotiation

Time
45 minutes

Procedure
Designate partners as A and B and have them role play all/any of the following situations. There may need to be some agreement on the context, but not too much pre-role play discussion.

1. A wants to go to the beach. B wants to go to the public swimming pool.
2. A wants to smoke. B doesn't, and doesn't want A to either.
3. A wants B to clean up the room.
4. A wants a date with B. B doesn't want to go.
5. B wants to 'nick' something from the store. A doesn't want to.
6. A wants to talk, B wants to go to sleep.
7. A has told the truth, but B doesn't believe them.
8. A wants to choose their own clothes, B doesn't want them to.

Discussion
- In how many situations did A change B's mind, and vice versa?
- How was this achieved?
- Is it always possible to negotiate a change of behaviour?
- What can you do if you can't negotiate?

133
Roads/Avenues

Focus
Minimal physical contact and feelings

Time
10 minutes

Procedure
1. Divide the group into even rows

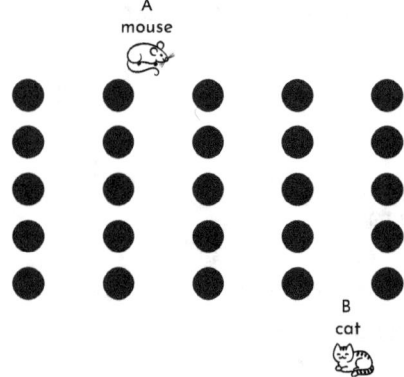

2. Choose one person to be a mouse (A) and one to be a cat (B). A and B stand in the positions shown.
3. A caller positions themselves at the front of the group. When they call 'Avenues', the group all extend their arms forward. When they call 'Roads', the group all extend one arm sideways.
4. The cat has to chase and catch the mouse, while the caller continually changes the directions of the roads and avenues that they can run along, to prevent the cat catching the mouse.
5. Change callers.

Discussion
(addressed only to the callers)
- How did you feel having all those people doing what you ordered?
- How did you feel if you let the cat catch the mouse?

(addressed to the group)
- How did you feel towards the person who let the cat catch the mouse?
- Was it really important?

134
Scissor Game

Focus
To develop perception and improve observation skills

Time
15 minutes

Materials
- Pair of scissors

Procedure
Designate partners as A and B and have them role play all/any of the following situations. There may need to be some agreement on the context but not too much pre-role play discussion.
1. A group of people are seated in a circle either on the floor or on chairs.
2. The group leader has a pair of scissors in their hands and passes them to the person on their right.
3. As they pass the scissors they say, 'I am passing them crossed' (or uncrossed). But they mean their legs, not the scissors. Keep passing around until someone guesses what is happening.
4. As each person passes the scissors around, they can open or close them or turn them over to focus attention on the scissors while saying "I am passing them…"

Discussion
- Discuss how you feel when:
    - You know the 'trick' to the game!
    - You don't understand what is going on!
- Discuss other times when you've been tricked!

135

Best Job

Focus
To develop perception and problem solving skills

Time
20 minutes

Materials
- Blindfolds, red and green stickers (dots)

Procedure
1. Divide into groups of three.
2. You must imagine that you have the opportunity to become secretary to a millionaire. The salary is 'ten times that of your wildest dreams', and the job is very interesting, involving lots of travel. Many brilliant people applied for the job but you three are the final bright, quick-thinking candidates.
3. Your prospective boss has set you a final test to decide the successful applicant.
4. You are blindfolded, and on your foreheads is placed a red or green dot.
5. The blindfolds are removed and after a minute you must raise your hand if you can see a red dot on either of the other candidates' heads.
6. After another minute, the first applicant to correctly tell the boss (the group leader) the colour of the dot on their own forehead and how they know, will get the job.

Solutions
Group leader should place either 2 red dots and 1 green dot per group, or 3 red dots per group. The solutions will become obvious if it is emphasised that everyone in the group is brilliant (therefore their reactions will provide clues for each other).

Discussion
- How did you feel when you solved the problem, or had not solved it when other people had?
- Were any combinations or positions more difficult than others? If so, which ones and why?

136
Predicament

Focus
Values clarification

Time
30 minutes

Procedure
1. One person is asked to leave the group.
2. Those remaining then decide on a predicament which they could be in.
3. The person out of the room will then be asked to come back in. They must attempt to find out the predicament. However, they may only ask the rest of the group the question 'what would you do in this predicament?'
4. They may ask anyone in the class as many times as they wish, until they discover the predicament.

Predicament examples:
a. You are at the beach swimming. When you come out of the water your clothes and money have been stolen. You live 40 kilometres away on the other side of town.
   John: 'Dave, what would you do in this predicament?'
   Dave: 'I would panic.'
   John: 'Mary, what would you do in this predicament?'
   Mary: 'I would lie in the sand.'
b. It is the day before your birthday and you have looked around the house and found your present on top of the wardrobe, but when you opened it up, it fell onto the ground and broke. It was a watch. What will you do?
c. You have found a five dollar note on the pavement. Just as you pick it up an old lady behind you says: 'Oh, thank you, I just dropped that out of my purse.'

Discussion

- Discuss the meaning of predicament. Find some common sayings for 'being in a predicament'. Usually, if you are 'in a predicament' it means you experience an inner conflict or dilemma and often don't want to hurt another person's feelings. Describe a predicament you were in, how you resolved it, then discuss alternative ways of solving the predicament.
- Is it always better to protect someone's feelings by not telling them the truth? Describe some situations.
- Discuss this statement: 'I should not take responsibility for someone else.' Does this mean you should always tell the truth to another person? Taking responsibility usually means using phrases like these:
    - 'He couldn't help it.'
    - 'I made them do it.'
    - 'She won't like that.'
    - 'I can tell what you are thinking.'

Make your own list.

137
Newspaper Costume

Focus
- To enable the group members to work together and make decisions
- To allow individual members to feel part of a group and to contribute ideas

Time
1 hour

Materials
- Bundles of newspaper and masking tape

Procedure
1. Have five people in each group.
2. Each team is given a bundle of newspaper and a roll of tape, and told to make the most creative costume possible for one member of the group.
3. 10 minutes is allowed for planning, during which time the paper and tape remain untouched. At the end of the planning time the groups have 10 minutes to make the costume.
4. At the end of this time everyone has a chance to look at other costumes and evaluate them. During this processing time ask such questions as:
   - 'Why was the wearer chosen?'
   - 'What could have been done to improve the team's effectiveness?'
   - 'How did the group feel when their costume was not judged the best?'
   - 'How did they feel if it was judged the best?'
   - 'What did the competitive feelings do to the team's effectiveness?'
5. After discussion, allow groups to repeat the activity using similar bundles of newspaper, and allow 15 minutes for planning the costume and 2 minutes to make it.

Discussion
- Did the teams work better the second time? What changed? Why?
- What factors contributed to the second design that were not present in the first?

138

Bomb Shelter

Focus
Values clarification and group decision making

Time
35 minutes

Procedure
1. Pick people to role play these ten citizens:
    - Policeman (with gun)
    - Professor
    - 3rd year medical student
    - Scientist
    - Chemist
    - Athlete
    - Priest
    - Pregnant woman (2 months)
    - Librarian (who is the pregnant women's husband)
    - Historian
2. Place the citizens in a circle on the floor and tell them they are in a bomb shelter.
3. Tell them that there is a nuclear war waging and that there is only enough food for 9 months for 5 people.
4. Tell them that 5 people must leave or they will all die. In order to evict anyone the whole group must agree on some leaving. Those leaving must be given a chance to present reasons why they shouldn't have to leave, but if everybody still agrees that they have to go, then they must leave.
5. The argument goes on until only 5 people are left.

Variation
1. Only 1 or 2 persons have to leave.
2. Even if the whole group decides one person must go, they don't have to go unless they want to. Discuss what you will do if no one wants to go.

Discussion
- Discuss how important some people are in certain situations, but in others are not much help: e.g. a doctor if their car breaks down, a mechanic if someone breaks a leg. Discuss what you can do about that in real life situations.
- Make a list of the things you can do well. Show it to a friend. Ask them if they agree. If they don't, ask why.
- Talk about your feelings when someone has made you feel useless, or stupid, or unhappy. Discuss the reasons why they might have done that.
- Discuss this statement: 'Nobody can make you feel embarrassed. You let yourself become embarrassed.'
- Talk about a situation in which you took responsibility for someone else and it was the wrong thing to do.

139
Passenger Balloon

Focus
Decision making, dilemmas and values

Time
30 minutes

Procedure
1. Pick 5 or 6 people to sit in a fairly small square which represents the basket of a passenger balloon. Each person has to pick an occupation for themselves, e.g. plumber, doctor, teacher, bricklayer, secretary, etc.
2. The balloon is slowly losing altitude and in order for some of the people to survive, one person has to jump out.
3. The people in the basket are given a set time limit of about 2 minutes to decide who has to jump out.
4. Everyone has to put forward an argument as to why they shouldn't have to jump out, and also say why someone else should. Everyone must agree on who has to jump out. If no one jumps out, everyone perishes.

Discussion
- Name some important people and say why they are considered important. Are they more important than you?
- Talk to a partner or friend about something that you really like or something that you are really interested in. See if you can get them interested as well. Switch.
- Is any one person more important than another? Is anybody in the room more important than you? Why? If yes, in what way?
- Talk about some of the ways some people try to show others how important they are. Perhaps if you have to keep showing people how important you are, you may not be that important after all.
- How can you become important? Do you want to? How did other people become important? Can you do it in the same way?
- How do we value ourselves for being who we are?

140
Life Boat

Focus
Self and values examination during decision making

Time
20 minutes

Procedure
1. Form a group of ten.
2. Each choose an occupation, e.g. journalist, plumber, bus driver etc. One person only to jump at a time.
3. Pretend you are all in a sinking life boat. The boat will sink and drown you all unless five people voluntarily jump overboard.
4. Each person thinks of an argument as to why they should not have to jump overboard.
5. Argue until all agree on which person should leave. This person must then jump overboard.
6. The game keeps going until only five people are left in the lifeboat.

Variation
1. The game goes on until only one person is left in the lifeboat.
2. Remove the rule that one person has to jump if all the others say so. They need only jump if they agree to do so.

Discussion
- Review the arguments put forward to decide who was to jump out of the life boat. Were they logical? Were they emotional? Were they practical?
- If you did the exercise again, what changes would you make to make it:
  - More interesting?
  - More difficult?
  - More fun?
  - More serious?
- Can you think of a situation where this activity might occur in real life? Do you think the real life activity would work out in the same way as the simulated activity?

141

Jury Service

Focus
Thinking logically

Time
30 minutes

Procedure
Set up a court of law, with someone (or a small group) as
- Defendant lawyer to prepare and present the case for the defender
- Crown lawyer to prepare and present the case for the crown
- Plaintiff to give evidence
- Prosecutor to give evidence against the defendant
- Jury to listen and adjudicate to give verdict
- Judge to sum up and make the judgement.

Is the defendant innocent, or guilty?

When the ice-cream shop proprietor came to work, they found the window of the shop smashed and a large container of strawberry ice-cream missing. The owner of the shoe shop opposite said they saw a white van driving hurriedly away at about seven o'clock after hearing a crashing sound, like glass breaking. The baker said they saw two men acting suspiciously at about 6.45 am outside the ice-cream shop. They had a torch, and were examining the lights of their van for quite some time. Later that morning the police found two men selling ice-cream at a fair from a white van. They showed the police a docket for the ice-cream and said that at 6.45 am they had been fishing. They showed the policeman that their fishing boat was still wet at home in their driveway. One of the men used to work for the ice-cream parlour.

Discussion
- Why lawyers are mostly used in a court of law, rather than the accused defending themselves.
- Circumstantial evidence. How influential is it in a court of law, the workplace, or ordinary living? Give examples.
- The jury system! Is it reliable? What system might be better? What are some of the problems with the use of a jury in a court of law? When is a jury not used and a judge alone makes a decision?

142

Lottery Week

Focus
Lateral thinking fantasy and values

Time
45 minutes

Procedure
1. Suddenly you have just won the million dollar lottery and you can do anything you want, money is unlimited for a week. Little do you know at the end of the week, the Lottery Club finds that you are not the winner. However, they let you keep what you have, and you don't have to pay anyone back.
2. Write down what you would do for five days of that week, beginning
   Day 1 ...
   Day 2 ...
   Day 3 ...

Discussion
- On another piece of paper write down what will happen to you when they take your money away from you, and you are back where you started, except for those things you bought and the experiences you had. Would you be a changed person? In what ways? Discuss.

143
Dear Heart Mender

Focus
Talking about problems and arriving at solutions

Time
45 minutes

Procedure
1. Write a letter to 'dear heart mender'. In this letter outline a problem that is worrying you. Try to make it a 'true to life' problem, rather than a fictional one, but one you are happy to disclose.
   Give the letter to your teacher or a partner, to make a reply. You could discuss the problem in a group, as well.
2. Sit in a circle. Tell the group about a problem of yours, or someone else's. It could be a problem at home or work, or it could be just something that isn't going right.
   e.g. 'I hate spinach, but mum keeps serving it to me.' or 'I am late for school because I can't get my little brother out of bed, and I have to take him to school.'
   Discuss in a group some possible solutions.

Discussion
- How can problems be solved so that all parties are satisfied?
- Which problems can be solved by yourself?

144
Personal Survey

Focus
To record answers to personal questions to ascertain if there are any patterns to your behaviour, for self-awareness and sharing

Time
45 minutes

Procedure
1. Rule three columns on a page. Write in the headings for each column:

Usually	Seldom	Sometimes

2. Answer each of the following questions honestly, by putting a mark in one of the columns. Think about each question.
   a. When you talk do the words come out the right way?
   b. Do people finish off sentences for you?
   c. Do you find it hard to talk with other people?
   d. Do you talk more than the other person in a conversation?
   e. When someone hurts your feelings do you talk to them about it?
   f. Do you apologise when you've hurt someone's feelings?
   g. Do you get upset when others disagree with you?
   h. Do you speak up when you think differently from the others?
   i. Do you sulk?
   j. Do you become shy when people give you a compliment?
   k. Do you try and cover up your faults from others?
   l. When talking do you let the other person finish before you start?
   m. Do others listen when you talk?
   n. Do you pretend to listen when you're not?
   o. Do you find it difficult to praise other people?

Discussion
- There are no correct answers. Survey your answers to see if you can discover a theme in the way that you deal with yourself and other people.
- Is there anything on your list that you would like to change? Discuss how you are going to change.

145

Do It

Focus
Group co-operation techniques

Time
1 hour

Procedure
1. Form groups of 3 or 4 and choose one of the activities from the list below.
   Write down how you would organise:
   - A disco
   - A BBQ
   - A concert
   - A soccer team
   - A class camp
   - A flower garden
   - A scone making group
   - A beach picnic
   - A hike and lunch
2. After 15 minutes, bring the groups together and discuss the groups arrangements. Discuss how the organisation and planning could lead to a successful outcome.
3. Actually implement one of the activities.

Discussion
- Review how the implementation corresponded to what was organised. What factors helped/hindered the successful implementation?

146

Grey Power

Focus
To show how people of different ages may have different values

Time
50 minutes

Procedure
1. Choose a group of friends with whom you can work well. Sit down with them, and write out a series of questions you could ask some senior citizens, or older people. You might ask:
'Where were you born?' 'Where were you brought up?' 'What kind of work did you do?' 'How many children did you have?' 'Where are your children now? And what are they doing?' 'What exciting experiences have you had?' 'What were your proudest moments?' 'What was your most embarrassing moment?' 'How do you use your time now?' etc.
2. The co-ordinator will need to discuss how a time and place can be organised for the group/individuals to ask someone those questions. E.g. call a senior citizens home, or stand in the street with a sign and wait for someone to come along. Ask them if they would mind if you asked some questions and indicate that it will take about twenty minutes. Thank the person for their time.

Discussion
- Discuss the answers to your questions in the group. Is there some way in which:
    - You can connect with and understand older people?
    - You can help the older people?
    - You can learn from older people and they can help you?

147
Camp Plan

Focus
Group co-operation practice

Time
45 minutes

Procedure
1. Discuss in groups how to organise a camp.
2. Write each of these headings on top of a page. Make sure you arrange all of these things:
   - Social activities
   - Learning or educational activities
   - Menu
   - Tours
   - Finances
   - Transport
   - Publicity
   - Accommodation
3. At the end of the session, present your plan to the other groups. Decide on the best plan. Go on a camp.

Discussion
- Spend a few minutes discussing how you made decisions. Was it by voting? Or agreement? Or someone shouting the loudest?
- Did the group work well together? How was this obvious to you? What could you do to get your group working better?
- After the camp, reflect on the planning process and the implementation process. What worked well and what was changed or added?

148
Animal Crackers

Focus
Group co-operation

Time
1 hour

Materials
- Oranges, potatoes, wood, pins, stapler, coloured paper, glue, lined paper, pens, magazines, scissors

Procedure

Animal Crackers
1. Form groups of six. Give each group an assortment of materials to work with.
2. Each group must make an animal, name it, and make up a story about the animal. Present your animal and story to the other groups.

Family Albums
1. Form groups of six. Give each group six pages. Write across the top of each sheet headings such as:
   - Being born
   - Childhood scenes
   - Marriage
   - Children
   - Holidays
   - Job
   - Sports etc.
2. Then give each group a number of magazines, and scissors and glue. From the magazines, each group has to build up a simulated family album.
3. Present your album to the rest of the groups.

Discussion
- What helped make this a pleasant/unpleasant activity?
- How could you have co-operated more to produce a better album?

149

Buzz Off

Focus
Group co-operation and competition

Time
20 minutes

Materials
- Beans, buttons or coins

Procedure
1. Make up two teams of three, each team sitting on one side of a table. Team A begins the game by hiding their hands under the table, and moving around a bean or button or coin amongst hands, until it rests in one hand. The captain says 'UP', and all the members of team place their clenched fists on the table in front of them.
2. Team B elects a captain, who begins to guess in which clenched fist the bean lies. They do this by pointing to a clenched fist, that they believe does not hold the bean, and say 'OFF'. If they are correct, and the hand is empty, it goes off and the score is 1. They continue adding 1 to their score every time they correctly guess an empty hand. If they choose the hand with the bean in it, the game is finished. Team B then hides the bean.
The winning team is the one with the greatest score before the bean is discovered.

Discussion
- How did you decide who was going to hold the bean?
- Did this procedure change? How was the captain elected? Do you think you could be elected captain in another situation?
- As the team with the bean, how did you act non-verbally to cooperate with your group and make it hard for the other group?
- In life, when are you both cooperating and competing?

150
Teacher For a Day

Focus
How to help someone

Time
40 minutes

Materials
- Cards, pen

Procedure
1. Make up a number of cards containing 3 or 4 simple facts, for instance:
    - Spelling cards containing ten words
    - Geography cards containing facts about a country
    - A poem
    - Instructions for making something.
2. Choose a partner, who is not your best friend. One person is to be the 'teacher', and the other the 'pupil'.
3. The 'teacher' selects a card from the information box. The 'teacher' has 5 minutes to teach the information to the 'pupil', test them on it, and make sure they get everything correct. Change roles and do the activity again.

Discussion
- Discuss different ways of teaching information.
- Discuss what to do if people do not understand immediately.
- When is 'help' unhelpful?

www.ingramcontent.com/pod-product-compliance
Lightning Source LLC
Chambersburg PA
CBHW050354120526
44590CB00015B/1691